KENT

of one hundred years ago

GROOMBRIDGE

WOMAN CARRYING WATER

KENT

of one hundred years ago

AYLWIN GUILMANT

First published in the United Kingdom in 1992 by
Alan Sutton Publishing Ltd · Phoenix Mill · Stroud · Gloucestershire

Copyright © Aylwin Guilmant 1992

Reprinted 1997

British Library Cataloguing in Publication Data
Guilmant, Aylwin
Kent of One Hundred Years Ago
I. Title
942.23081

ISBN 0-7509-0156-X

Library of Congress Cataloging in Publication Data applied for

LIFEBOAT SATURDAY, SITTINGBOURNE

Endpapers, Front: F. Durrant, Grocer, Sandwich. Back: High Street, Rochester.

Typeset in 11/13 Bembo
Typesetting and origination by
Alan Sutton Publishing Limited.
Printed and bound in Great Britain by
WBC, Bridgend, Mid Glam.

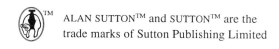

ALAN SUTTON™ and SUTTON™ are the
trade marks of Sutton Publishing Limited

Preface

I'm just in love with all these three,
The Weald and the Marsh and the Down countrie;
Nor I don't know which I love the most,
The Weald or the Marsh or the white chalk coast!

I've buried my heart in a ferny hill,
Twix' a liddle low shaw an' a great high gill.
Oh hop-bine yaller and woodsmoke blue,
I reckon you'll keep her middling true!

I've loosed my mind for to out and run,
On a Marsh that was old when Kings begun;
Oh Romney level and Brenzett reeds,
I reckon you know what my mind needs!

I've given my soul to the Southdown grass,
And sheep-bells tinkled where you pass
Oh Firle an' Ditchling an' sails at sea,
I reckon you keep my soul for me!

Who is more qualified to speak in praise of Kent than Rudyard Kipling, a resident of Sussex, who in the above 'Three-Part Song' from *Puck of Pook's Hill* displayed his love and knowledge of both counties, Sussex and Kent, a land apart. Throughout the ages they have been linked in so many ways, especially by their common boundary, which is often so difficult to define accurately that some guidebooks of the last century claimed that Rye was sited in Kent and Tunbridge Wells in Sussex!

People living at the opening of the twentieth century saw many changes, in particular the exodus from rural areas to the towns. The aim of this book is to present a picture of the past, not of the well-born, of whom there were many in Kent, but of the ordinary man and woman whose daily lives were often passed in conditions far from ideal. The County of Kent is a land of contrasts from the Weald to the marshes, the North Downs to the sea; from those whose working lives were in industries, agriculture or fishing, the pictures remind us of their hardships and simple pleasures.

SMALLHYTHE

1

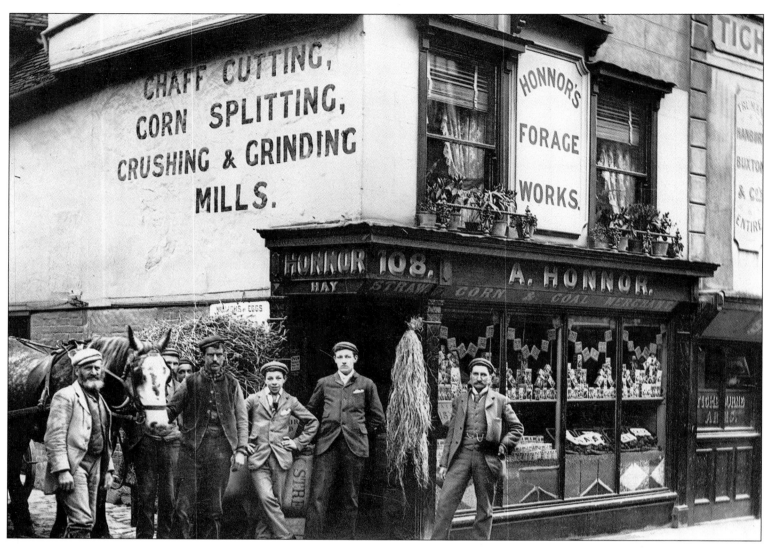

MAIDSTONE

The photographs are mainly from the years 1880–1920, and the text, both fact and fiction, is contemporary with them; a tribute to those writers of another age who lived in and loved this land. It must be stressed that some of the pictures may show people and places both sides of the Kent and Sussex boundary, for who can say which part of a country lane or marshland stream may lie across the border. Pictures of Deptford, Greenwich and Woolwich are included too, as they were in Kent until 1888, when the County of London swallowed them up.

Although the picture we have of life at the turn of the century is coloured by our realization that it was a 'golden age' before the devastation of the First World War, it was not as idyllic as it sometimes appears. A farm labourer's life would have been long and arduous, particularly for waggoners who were responsible for the horses in their team. After a hard day's work in the field, certain duties would have had to be carried out in the stable, and a fifteen-hour day was not unusual. Wages were low and agricultural cottages 'tied' so that there was often little alternative to the workhouse at the end of a working life. The 'grim reaper' showed no mercy to either rich or poor, however, and infant mortality was the scourge of all classes.

The urban classes were considerably better off than their rural counterparts. Regular work in industry paid a good basic wage, and enabled a great proportion of the population to enjoy an annual holiday, or to take advantage of railway excursions. The seaside resorts expanded enormously at this time, as popular railway travel enabled many people to have much more mobility than before.

A book of this nature has only been made possible by the generosity of museums, libraries, local history societies and the many individuals who have made available their collections of photographs, many taken by local people, and of local people.

Below the down the stranded town
Hears far away the rollers beat;
About the wall the seabirds call;
The salt wind murmurs through the street;
Forlorn the sea's forsaken bride
Awaits the end that shall betide.

John Davidson

2

Introduction

Kent is in the extreme south-eastern corner of England at the point nearest to the continent; consequently it has been a place of great historical importance from earliest times. It is bounded on two sides by the sea, and on the north by the River Thames. At the beginning of this century, Kent was one of the twelve largest counties in England.

Nature has marked Kent into three distinct divisions, the great range of chalk hills, known as the North Downs, the wide sea and river marshes, and the fruitful Weald. It has been said that no English county offers a greater variety of attractive scenery than that of Kent.

While many regard Kent as the cornerstone of the kingdom, it has been the scene of some of the most noteworthy events in our history. The first landing place of Julius Caesar and his Roman army, it was subsequently invaded and settled by Hengest and Horsa, leaders of the Jutes, and when St Augustine landed in England it was in Kent that he first set foot. Today the county boasts not only Canterbury cathedral but also another fine one, at Rochester.

Kent has always been in a favourable position for trade and commerce. Close to London and served by the Roman road of Watling Street, the shortest route from the Continent to the capital runs through the county. Its proximity to London was a further reason for its early development. Good communications by sea were another advantage and Kent's numerous ports still have a large and increasing trade.

The river most characteristic of Kent is the Medway. Entering the county at the Sussex border, it meanders in a north-easterly direction, passing through many of the ancient towns before it reaches Sheerness and the estuary of the Thames. Edmund Spenser wrote:

> The salt Medway that trickling streams
> Adorn the dales of Kent
> Till with his elder brother Thames
> His brackish waves be blent.

COTTAGE NEAR HORSMONDEN

3

For much of its total length of sixty miles the Medway was navigable, while the valley of the Medway was one of the earliest places of settlement, home to Neolithic man, and subsequently favoured by people of both the Bronze and Iron age.

Much has been made of the question of racial origin and dialect within Kent, and some people believe that the old dialect can be traced back to the Saxon invaders of the fifth and sixth centuries. East of the Medway we speak of 'A man of Kent', while one who dwells on the west of that river is called 'A Kentish man', and it is believed that this distinction dates from the time when there were two kingdoms in Kent, one with its capital at Canterbury, and the other at Rochester.

In 1051 the men of Dover were involved in an affray with Count Eustace of Boulogne. As a result of this, Earl Godwin and his son, Harold, clashed with King Edward and were obliged to seek sanctuary abroad. In 1052 however, the earl landed at Dungeness where he received promises of support from men in Kent, Sussex and Surrey. Peace was restored between the king and Godwin, and Norman influence in England was soon at its lowest ebb. Harold claimed the throne in 1066, following the death of the king, but the peace was fragile and Harold was involved in subduing more northern parts of his kingdom. William of Normandy landed at this time, and was victorious at the Battle of Hastings. William recognized the strategic importance of keeping open his most direct link with Normandy, so advanced along the south coast. He met with resistance at Romney but Dover surrendered on demand; from there he travelled to Canterbury. While William was there he negotiated with other important places in southern England. On receiving submission from the men of Kent, he granted them recognition of their old customs and laws. The most distinctive of these was Gavelkind, the name given to the primary system of land tenure in Kent. By this law, land was divided equally on a man's death between his sons, while a widow was entitled to a dower in one-half of her late husband's land.

Domesday Book shows how Kent was divided into seven large divisions called lathes, which were in turn subdivided into hundreds. The lathes of Kent compare with the rapes of Sussex. Domesday also gives details of the ownership of the larger estates in the county, the greatest landowner being King William himself. In accordance with his policy of giving land to his Norman followers, William conferred the earldom of Kent on Odo, Bishop of Bayeux. Both the Archbishop of Canterbury and the Bishop of Rochester owned land on a more modest scale.

The towns on the Kent coast were extremely important in view of the continental traffic; they were also England's first line of defence against invasion. The five main towns of the south-east, subsequently known as the 'Cinque Ports' were (except for Hastings) in Kent. They and their 'limbs' were granted charters confirming their special rights and privileges, among them exemption from taxation and the power to set up their own courts of law. In exchange, the ports were assigned certain duties to be performed when the king demanded, also to offer ship-service whenever necessary and to repel pirates. It has been claimed that the Fleet they maintained was the forerunner of the British navy. The ports reached their zenith of power during the latter half of the thirteenth century, but this waned following the great storms which left many stranded some miles from the sea, and altered the course of rivers.

The prosperity of the Kentish yeoman is proverbial, partially based on the security of tenure and the aforementioned system of gavelkind. This level of well-being was further enhanced during the reign of Edward III, who was responsible for introducing the weaving industry into the county. The richness of agricultural land should not be overlooked, however, for as the old rhyme states:

LEEDS CASTLE

A knight of Cales,
A gentleman of Wales,
And a Laird of the North Countree;
A yeoman of Kent,
With his yearly rent,
Will buy 'em out all three.

Kent was one of the half-dozen counties in which the hop was grown commercially. The hop gardens, together with rich stretches of cherry and apple orchards, are characteristic of the county and are a major part of its agricultural wealth.

Following the plague, or 'Black Death', in the fourteenth century, the peasantry began to demand more religious and political freedom. The rising in 1381 had many causes, one of which was the poll-tax levied to pay for the interminable war with the French, who raided Kent on a number of occasions. The meeting of Wat Tyler and the young King Richard II is too well known to require further explanation. Despite the promise made by the king some rioters suffered prosecution, and many towns throughout the length and breadth of the county were adversely affected before peace was restored. Jack Cade's rebellion of the next century was a far more serious threat, as a different stratum of society took up arms. Again this rebellion was crushed, and pardon was granted to many of the malcontents.

Following the murder of Thomas à Becket at Canterbury Cathedral in the twelfth century, the place became a place of pilgrimage, and remained so until the dissolution of the monasteries by Henry VIII. It was at this time that the king built a series of blockhouses around the Kentish coast in anticipation of a Roman Catholic invasion from the continent. On Henry's death, Mary Tudor came to the throne; when she married Philip of Spain (a fellow Catholic) Sir Thomas Wyatt took up arms. It may be because of his action that Kent suffered much during the Marian persecutions, when many protestant 'heretics' were burnt at the stake. However, when Queen Elizabeth I came to the throne, she not only crushed the might of the Spanish armada, but was also instrumental in founding the royal dockyard at Chatham, thus enhancing the importance of Kent.

During the Civil War, the county was divided in its loyalties. Kentish Royalists were repelled at Maidstone, while Dover Castle was held for Parliament. At the Restoration Charles II landed at Dover, where he was welcomed by the people, while James II set sail from Sheerness in his first attempt to flee the country. In the seventeenth century parts of the county suffered attacks from the Dutch, the fort at Sheerness was destroyed, while Chatham and Gravesend were both in the front line.

Kent industries expanded during the period of continental discontent, when many refugees came into the county. The local ironworkings had flourished from Tudor times in the Weald; this was brought about as both the ore and the fuel (charcoal) were readily obtainable. Transportation was a problem, though, particularly for such a heavy commodity as iron. While the Wealden roads were somewhat better than those in Sussex, they were nevertheless far from ideal, but Kent was fortunate in having a number of navigable waterways.

Clothmaking in and around Cranbrook grew partly because of the flocks of sheep on Romney Marsh, but also because water-power and fuller's earth were readily available. Kentish broadcloth was much in demand both for the home market and abroad. Silk-weavers from the continent settled in Canterbury, while papermaking, which again was started by a German refugee, flourished at Dartford. All these people of foreign extraction aided the prosperity of the county.

During this same period many of the people of Kent gained their livelihood from agriculture or associated occupations. Orchards increased in number, while the introduction of the vine in the sixteenth century was an added bonus:

> Hops and pickerel, carp and beer,
> Came into England all in a year.

So runs one of the many versions of an old rhyme, which may not be strictly true. Since its introduction the hop has so flourished that in many places it grows wild.

Market-gardening was started in the Sandwich area by the Walloons, who subsequently became known as 'the Dutchmen'. The growing of vegetables became popular, and cabbages and carrots found a ready market in London, where the fashion took hold.

A 17 lb CABBAGE

CUTTING WOOD

Again, the close proximity to London favoured the quarrying of stone and the allied manufacture of bricks and tiles. This, together with the expanding royal dockyards at Deptford, Woolwich and Chatham brought prosperity to the north of the county in particular.

The fishing industry remained in a relatively prosperous state throughout the centuries, it has only declined to the position it holds today within the last hundred years.

As befits a county wealthy both in industries and agriculture many towns sprang up; those in the Weald were involved in the clothmaking industry and were also market towns, while the coastal ones acted as points of both import and export. The expansion of towns inevitably led to the need for more schools, the two oldest surviving being King's School, Canterbury and King's School, Rochester, both associated with their respective cathedrals. Other schools date back to the fifteenth century, and many were endowed by wealthy merchants.

Kent's early history and geographical setting brought about a rich variety of domestic architecture. The 'Wealden' house of the yeoman of Kent is legendary, while large country houses came to take the place of the fortified house and castle, of which there are many, in particular the three Norman castles along the strategic line of Watling Street. It is believed that the close proximity of London was a further source of Kent's early development, as well-to-do merchants had their country seats there. Penshurst, for example, was originally the residence of a lord mayor of London. During the eighteenth century, money from commerce rather than agriculture was utilized to further improve these properties. Many of the owners were quick to see that a well-designed park and garden would complement their seat. The landscape architect 'Capability' Brown is credited with designing the park of Leeds Castle.

A WAGONER AND TEAM

CHURCH HILL, BECKENHAM

Together with the rest of the country, Kent suffered a depression in agriculture following the Napoleonic wars, but reached a height of prosperity in the middle of the nineteenth century. With the exception of dairy-farming, agriculture again slumped.

The population of Kent continued to grow at this time, particularly in the most industrialized areas of north-west and north Kent. Population in many of the villages was depleted, as migration to the towns took place. Only where they had a local industry or were close to towns with a labour shortage did villages prosper. Wages for agricultural workers were low in comparison with other parts of the country in 1800 – £12–£15 a year plus board for a single labourer 'living-in', while a married labourer, living in a rented cottage costing £2 or £3 a year, would earn 2s. to 2s. 6d. for a ten-hour day. Cobbett, who toured Kent in 1823, also mentions great poverty, particularly in the eastern part of the county. It is believed that this was one of the underlying causes of the 'Swing' riots which affected much of Kent, before spreading to Sussex and neighbouring counties. Originally, inadequate labourers' wages had been supplemented from the poor rate, but following the report of a Royal Commission which was set up to enquire into the administration of the Poor Law, reform took place. According to Jessup, writing in *A History of Kent*, however, 'its efficiency was of a mechanistic kind, and its inhuman administration was one of the causes that led to the extraordinary Courtenay rising in 1838 . . .' Courtenay was mentally unstable, but stirred up trouble within the county before his untimely end.

ASLEEP IN THE HOP GARDEN

The development of the railways further enhanced the prosperity of Kent. They gave employment to a great number of the labouring class, linked much of the county with the capital and opened up the seaside resorts. The population of these coastal towns rose considerably – Margate, for example, from just under 5,000 at the opening of the nineteenth century to five times that figure within a hundred years.

By the beginning of the twentieth century, although Kent was not in any sense a manufacturing county like Yorkshire or Lancashire, there were some important industries. Shipbuilding gave employment to a large number of men at Chatham, Rochester, Gillingham and Sheerness, while the Royal Dockyards were also important centres. At Erith (on the Thames) electrical apparatus was manufactured, and at Ashford the works of the South-Eastern and Chatham Railway made railway coaches and wagons. Gunpowder was produced in many places, bricks were made at Sittingbourne, Milton and Faversham, while stone was worked by a substantial number of masons at Maidstone. During the same period, nearly 5,000 people in Kent were engaged in the manufacture of paper. Some large towns had their own breweries, while jam-making on a commercial basis increased, following the rise in fruit growing. The county thus in a short space of time went from mainly an agricultural one to a more industrialized state. Coal was discovered in 1891 by borings made from the abandoned workings for the projected nineteenth-century Channel tunnel, but it is believed that inadequate means of transport handicapped this industry in its early stage.

Throughout its history Kent has been in the forefront of battle, particularly during the Napoleonic wars. Defences were strengthened along the coastline with the building of the Martello towers, three further forts were built at Chatham, military camps were established over much of the county, while the Royal Military Canal, running from Hythe to Rye, formed a further barrier. At the outbreak of the First World War, the ports of Kent were places of embarkation for the troops on their way to the Western Front. As a result the county suffered some shelling from German shipping, but this was slight by comparison with the bombing of the Second World War. The threat of invasion was as great in 1940 as it had been early in the 1800s, and the coastal defences were strengthened once again. Much of the civilian population was evacuated from the seaside towns and inland villages, and barricades were erected along the beaches. Kent was directly underneath the German bombers *en route* to London, and the aerial Battle of Britain was fought mainly over the county and the Thames Estuary.

The development of motor transport and the consequent new network of roads has further increased the importance of Kent. Although the railways link the ports with places inland, today intercontinental travel has been facilitated by the building of motorways and will further be enhanced with the construction of the Channel Tunnel. Within the space of a century Kent has gone from an agricultural county of small market towns and coastal resorts, to become a place of industry, but also one of passage and transmigration.

MARGATE

KENT

of one hundred years ago

TENTERDEN BREWERY.
WINE AND SPIRIT STORES.

O. EDWARDS & SONS,
(LATE R. C. M. YOUNG.)

GENUINE HOME BREWED FAMILY ALES

per gallon.

Superior Family Bitter Ales	XXX	1	6
Ditto Mild	XXX	1	6
Ditto Mild	XX	1	4
Ditto Mild Beer	X	1	0
Bitter Beer	X	1	0
Ditto T Beer			10
SS Stout		1	6
— Stout		1	4
London Porter		1	0
Table Beer			8

WINES & SPIRITS OF THE BEST QUALITY

per gallon.

Jersey Brandy	2	6
Best Cognac Brandy (pale or brown)	4	6
Best Unsweetened Gin	2	6
Finest Old Tom Gin	2	3
Royal Highland Whisky	3	6
Finest Irish Malt Ditto	3	6
Old Jamaica Rum	3	6
Ditto	2	6
Best Cordial Gin	2	0

ALL ORDERS PROMPTLY ATTENDED TO.
All Wines of the best quality at the lowest possible Prices.

MILSTED

THE KENTISH VILLAGES

We are reminded by Mr F's aunt, in *Little Dorrit*, that 'there are milestones on the Dover Road,' but in the age of railways, until the incoming of cycles and motor cars, only few people saw them. The 20th-century invasion of the rural districts, rendered easy by new methods of locomotion, has brought to light many a quaint and curious place that has long been neglected. One of the most effective ways to see village life in Kent is to take a bicycle tour of several days, and for choice the locality selected should be in the eastern part of the county, for there not only will rural life be found unadulterated with town manners, but also nearly every village in that part of the county is full of traditions of events of great national interest. For instance, start from Dover, striking into one of the inland roads, in the direction that the Romans took in passing between Dover and Richborough. Having reached the Greater Stour, visit the villages on its southern bank. Then the series of village centres which occupy the slopes of the Elham Valley may be taken, until, reaching the Folkestone Plain, where, nestling at the foot of the chain of hills, are several places full of old-world interest extending right up to the verge of Romney Marsh westward, while others margin the old Roman road called Stone Street, which runs direct as an arrow's flight from Lympne Hill to Canterbury. Zig-zag back through Smeeth, Brabourne and Aldington, the line of the Royal Military Canal leads on to Appledore, where a most interesting line of country runs up to Tenterden, a charmingly sequestered place from whence a chain of villages supply connecting links with Ashford and the Great Stour Valley, by Chilham and Chatham back to Canterbury. But a bird-like flight and a bird's-eye view of these village centres will not suf-fice; we must individualise and sample them to get their flavour. We hear much of the decay of the villages, of the drifting of rural populations into towns, and this is alleged to be due to the unbearable dulness of village life. A glance at the village census returns taken at the opening of the 20th century leaves no doubt but that the natural increase of the village population is migrating into the towns, while the villages, from generation to generation, remain stationary or slowly decline; but it is not proven that this arises from the dulness of rural life. To those who have never spent a night beyond range of lamplight and cannot exist without the stimulant of successive editions of morning and evening newspapers, supplemented by telegrams and telephones, village life may seem tame, but the genuine and most successful villager can do with a very small allowance of these luxuries, because he comes in closer touch with nature than his neighbours of the towns. The scent of the freshly mown hay and the newly turned furrow are grateful to him; he is interested in the hills, vales and streams, all of which have their special associations, while the parish church, which is usually the most ancient fabric in a village, is always a centre of social and historic interest. If we made a tour of the villages of east Kent simply for the sake of seeing its churches the excursion would well repay us, because in many cases they are ancient monuments of much importance, forming links with the distant past when Kent was an independent kingdom. . . .

The Kentish villages are unquestionably very pleasant places in which to spend a summer's day or to sojourn in for a week or a fortnight 'when the bloom is on the rye'. They are good places into which to go as visitors to spend the money earned elsewhere, but the question is, What sort of places are they for summer and winter, and to earn a living in? Judged from the

SISSINGHURST

LYDD

census figures the answer cannot be entirely satisfactory. The general stagnation, and, in some cases, the marked decline in population, suggests that there is something wrong with the villages. Take a typical case. The town of Dover is increasing in population by leaps and bounds, yet in the last ten years the purely rural villages of the Dover Union, with a population of less than 7,000, showed a decrease of 361; and out of the twenty-four rural districts of Kent fourteen of them show a decrease during the last ten years, and on examining the returns from the separate parishes in the ten rural districts which show an increase, the growth is found to be entirely in parishes which impinge on urban areas. At the last census 214 rural parishes of Kent – fully two-thirds of the whole – showed a decreased population, and it being a fact that in each one of those parishes the birth rate exceeded the death rate it is evident that there is going on a continual migration from the villages to the towns and to other lands. It should be remembered that the greater part of those who leave the rural parishes are neither children nor old people. Many thousands of the flower of the populations of these villages have, during the last ten years, gone away – not into the next parish, but into the towns or entirely out of the country. Why have they gone? In some a restless disposition no doubt led them to seek new lands, but the great majority of English people have an overpowering love for their native place, and nothing but stern necessity would induce them to leave it. Why have they left it?

MARDEN

Some say it is for lack of houses, but that is only in exceptional cases; there are in the rural districts of Kent between four or five thousand houses uninhabited, showing that the supply far exceeds the demand. The plain truth seems to be that the ambitious and enterprising young people are leaving the villages because they can see no prospect of earning a living there. Agriculture is still the staple rural occupation, and in wandering through parish after parish it is surprising how few people can be seen working on the land, yet considering how sparsely the rural places are populated it is not so very surprising. Taking the whole of the rural districts of Kent and comparing the acres with the population, we find that if the whole of the people turned out – old and young – men, women and children, there would only be one to every three acres, and in some of the parishes there would only be a dot of humanity on each fifteen acres.

T. Bavington Jones

THE RAMSGATE TRAWLER

Of all the ships that may be seen round our coasts few can compare with the sailing trawler; strong and picturesque, these boats win their hard living in the rough seas that surround our shores.

There are now only three ports where the sailing trawler may be seen in numbers; Brixham, Lowestoft, and Ramsgate, where there are 190 boats; at all times some of these may be seen, re-fitting, landing fish, and best of all, a fleet of them putting to sea. In the calm summer their ruddy brown sails make contrast to the blue sky, reflect again into the shining water and make pictures lovely to see; but this is not the trawlers' weather, they like a 'stiff breeze', or the landsman might call it a gale. At such times their speed in sailing is wonderful; with a reef in the mainsail, perhaps they rush through the seas, spray and water dashing over their decks, the white foam clearing from their bows; they are as things alive under the control of their hardy skippers.

Their names are interesting and varied, many of them very appropriate, such as *Industry* and *Resolute*, others have a bearing on the lady friends of their owners or skippers, such as *True Love*, *Florrie*, and *Susie*, there are also the *Cherub*, *Early Dawn*, *Sea Flower*, *Fiery Cross*, and *Norman Craig*, the *Otter* and *Alfred*, both of fame as life-savers. There is no end to the possibility of a smack's name.

Their tonnage is about 25 to 42 tons, and length from 50 to 63 feet. They are ketch-rigged, and known variously as smacks, dandies, or trawlers.

The fishing is done by means of a beam trawl; this is, roughly speaking, a triangular bag of net kept open at the top by a beam about forty feet long with iron heads, the bottom being kept open by a ground rope; the cod or narrow end of the net is tied while trawling. The boat tows the trawl, the ground rope of which, dragging over the sea-bed, disturbs the fish that live in the sand at the bottom causing them to rise about a foot in the water, thus getting caught up in the net. After about six hours' towing the net is hauled on board, the cod end untied, and the fish emptied on to the deck. The best weather for this work is a 'stiff breeze', for the net retards the boat's way by as much as six or seven miles an hour, and unless she can tow it at the rate of from two to three miles an hour the net cannot be kept properly open and free from chafe.

RAMSGATE HARBOUR

The bulk of the fish caught by the Ramsgate boats are landed at that port, the greater part of which are sent all over the district and to London; but at times, when it is very rough in the North, the prime fish is sent to Grimsby. The fish market presents an animated scene in the early morning.

The smaller boats do most of their fishing round the Goodwin Sands and off the North and South Forelands, but the larger ones fish mostly in the North Sea.

Their crews vary from three men and a boy in the larger boats to two men and a boy in the smaller ones. This means heavy work even with their steam capstan, which they use to haul in the trawl and to warp their boat along in the harbour. The crews have to work hard and put up with rough times, but this makes 'men' and 'sailors', and there are none better in the world. Occasionally they are able to render assistance to craft less seaworthy than themselves; if this results in saving the boat they may get some well-earned salvage money. The doings of the *Otter* and the *Alfred* may give some idea of this.

One fearful December night off the Thames Estuary the *Otter* was making her way home with three reefs in her mainsail, and fell in with a schooner which signalled distress. All through the night the smack stood by, and as soon as it was possible got two of her men on board to help the schooner's crew, who were hard pressed. They got a rope across to the smack, which tried to tow the schooner to Lowestoft. All through the day, in a still very stiff gale, they kept to it, but when near the port the wind veered round, and back they were driven for another night off the Thames Estuary; no

sleep, and with scarcely any food left, they battled on with the gale. Finally, on the Sunday, the wind fell, and the *Otter* and her prize were off Ramsgate and near to safety, when the towing rope broke; but another trawler came to her assistance, and together they brought in the schooner.

The *Alfred* was one of the fleet caught by the disastrous gale of the autumn of 1911, when three of the Ramsgate boats were lost with all their crew; she had weathered the first part of the gale when she fell in with the *Gratitude* of Lowestoft, a sailing trawler dismasted and unmanageable, with only two of her crew left; the two survivors had little chance of seeing home again. One of the *Alfred's* crew managed at great risk to get across to the *Gratitude* with a rope, and get her in tow. She was finally brought into Lowestoft; later the *Alfred's* crew were noticed by the Royal Humane Society. The trawler *Concord* was the means of bringing ashore the crew, dog, cat, and canary of an Italian steamship, which foundered off the Goodwins.

Years ago there was a good bit of ill feeling between the French fishermen and our own portsmen and fights were not infrequent. As the French drifter usually carries about 15 hands and our trawlers 3 to 5, sometimes our boats got carried into Boulogne or Gravelenge, sometimes it was the reverse. The story goes that one skipper of a Ramsgate boat, with a sense of humour and the picturesque, met with the following adventure: For some reason or other a French boat ranged alongside and 8 of her crew boarded the English boat; her skipper had an old pistol with which he held the boarders at

DEAL

bay, and being handy with his ship sheered off, put the Frenchmen under hatches and brought them into Ramsgate, charging them with attempted piracy on the high seas.

Several years ago there was a big fight in Ramsgate, which caused considerable excitement in the place. The following is vouched for: During the time of the South African war one of our boats was fishing off the Varne Sands, near by was a French steam line fisher; when the English boat hauled up her trawl the Frenchmen bore down, pretending their gear had been damaged, intending to board and carry our boat to France. The skipper had no intention of allowing this, and leaving the trawl with the crew went to meet the boarders with a handspike, and dared them to come on; he looked so determined they sheered off. In reporting the matter he said to the owner, 'You know, gov'nor, I'd have killed every man of them before I'd gone to France;' and the owner considers him a man of his word.

There are several quaint and strange superstitions lingering amongst these sailors, the origin of which are hard to trace.

Ease and luxury are not a part of the trawler's life; it makes brave and strong men, as good to carry on the traditions of our motto as any within the country.

'Hal' O'Thanet

TERMINATIONS

One early-closing evening in July they left the baby to the servant cousin, and Kipps took Ann for a row on the Hythe canal. The sun set in a mighty blaze, and left a world warm, and very still. The twilight came. And there was the water, shining bright, and the sky a deepening blue, and the great trees that dipped their boughs towards the water, exactly as it had been when he paddled home with Helen, when her eyes seemed to him like dusky stars. He had ceased from rowing and rested on his oars, and suddenly he was touched by the wonder of life – the strangeness that is a presence stood again by his side.

Out of the darkness beneath the shallow, weedy stream of his being rose a question, a question that looked up dimly and never reached the surface. It was the question of the wonder of the beauty, the purposeless, inconsecutive beauty, that falls so strangely among the happenings and memories of life. It never reached the surface of his mind, it never took to itself substance or form; it looked up merely as the phantom of a face might look, out of deep waters, and sank again into nothingness.

'Artie,' said Ann.

He woke up and pulled a stroke. 'What?' he said.

15

HYTHE CANAL

'Penny for your thoughts, Artie.'

He considered.

'I reely don't think I was thinking of anything,' he said at last, with a smile. 'No.'

He still rested on his oars.

'I expect,' he said, 'I was thinking jest what a Rum Go everything is. I expect it was something like that.'

'Queer old Artie!'

'Ain't I? I don't suppose there ever was a chap quite like me before.'

He reflected for just another minute.

'Oo! – I dunno,' he said at last, and roused himself to pull.

H.G. Wells

MARRIAGE CUSTOM AT CRANBROOK

It is customary here when a newly-married couple leave the church to strew the pathway – not with flowers, but with the emblems of the bridegroom's calling. For example – Carpenters walk on shavings; butchers on skins of slaughtered sheep; the followers of St Crispin are honoured with leather parings; paper-hangers with strips of paper; blacksmiths with old iron, etc. In other parishes in this county, however, butchers are favoured with 'Rough Music', made from marrowbones and cleavers, printers from 'chases' (the technical term for the iron framework which encloses the types from which the impression in printing obtained).

The Kentish Note Book

LIKE LEVIATHANS AFLOAT

Descending Stroud Hill, we find ourselves at the foot of Rochester Bridge, and see before us the glittering Medway, and beyond, the grim keep of the old fortress, and the tall tower of the Cathedral springing out of a mass of many-coloured roofs. The view from this point is very striking. 'How solemn,' says Mr D. Radcliffe, 'the appearance of the Castle, with its square ghastly walls, and their hollow eyes rising over the right bank of the Medway, gray, and massive, and floorless – nothing remaining but the shell.' The river runs clear and limpid, save where the shadows rest upon it of huge dismasted men-of-war, 'laid up in ordinary', or stately screw steam-ships, which

> Like Leviathans afloat,
> Lay their bulwarks on the brine.

A curious combination the twofold scene presents of rural landscapes 'above bridge', and military pomp and pride below. Here the eye rests on smiling meadows and rich masses of foliage; there on the long lines of the buildings of the Arsenal, vast building-slips, and chalk-hills crowned with defensive works.

An eminent hand, one of 'the celebrities' of Rochester, has transferred the picture before us to the immortal pages of *The Pickwick Papers*, as it presented itself to the admiring gaze of Mr Pickwick.

> On the left of the spectator lay a ruined wall, broken in many places, and in some, overhanging the narrow

16

ROCHESTER

beach below in rude and heavy masses. Huge knots of sea-weed hung upon the jagged and pointed stones, trembling in every breath of wind; and the green ivy hung mournfully round the dark and ruined battlements. Behind it rose the ancient castle, its towers roofless, and its massive walls crumbling away, but telling us proudly of its old might and strength, as when, 700 years ago, it rang with the clash of arms, or resounded with the noise of feasting and revelry. On either side, the banks of the Medway, covered with corn-fields and pastures, with here and there a windmill, or a distant church, stretched away as far as the eye could see, presenting a rich and varied landscape, rendered more beautiful by the changing shadows which passed swiftly across it, as the thin and half-formed clouds skimmed away in the light of the morning sun. The river, reflecting the clear blue of the sky, glistened and sparkled as it flowed noiselessly on; and the oars of the fishermen dipped into the water with a clear and liquid sound, as the heavy but picturesque boats glided slowly down the stream.

But let us cross the bridge, and enter Rochester.

Black's Guide to Kent

ROCHESTER CASTLE

17

A DYKE ON ROMNEY MARSH

DYMCHURCH FLIT

They came down, and as Hobden opened the shutter to see if the potatoes were done Tom Shoesmith said to the children, 'Put a plenty salt on 'em. That'll show you the sort o' man I be.' Again he winked, and again the Bee Boy laughed and Una stared at Dan.

'I know what sort o' man you be,' old Hobden grunted, groping for the potatoes round the fire.

'Do ye?' Tom went on behind his back. 'Some of us can't abide Horseshoes, or Church Bells, or Running Water; an', talkin' o' runnin' water' – he turned to Hobden, who was backing out of the roundel – 'd'you mind the great floods at Robertsbridge, when the miller's man was drowned in the street?'

'Middlin' well.' Old Hobden let himself down on the coals by the fire door. 'I was courtin' my woman on the Marsh that year. Carter to Mus' Plum I was, gettin' ten shillin's week. Mine was a Marsh woman.'

'Won'erful odd-gates place – Romney Marsh,' said Tom Shoesmith. 'I've heard say the world's divided like into Europe, Ashy, Afriky, Ameriky, Australy, an' Romney Marsh.'

'The Marsh folk think so,' said Hobden. 'I had a hem o' trouble to get my woman to leave it.'

'Where did she come out of? I've forgot, Ralph.'

'Dymchurch under the Wall,' Hobden answered, a potato in his hand.

'Then she'd be a Pett – or a Whitgift, would she?'

'Whitgift.' Hobden broke open the potato and ate it with the curious neatness of men who make most of their meals in the blowy open. 'She growed to be quite reasonable-like after

WITTERSHAM

BROOKLAND CHURCH

livin' in the Weald awhile, but our first twenty year or two she was odd-fashioned, no bounds. And she was a won'erful hand with bees.' He cut away a little piece of potato and threw it out to the door.

'Ah! I've heard say the Whitgifts could see further through a millstone than most,' said Shoesmith. 'Did she, now?'

'She was honest-innocent of any nigromancin',' said Hobden. 'Only she'd read signs and sinnifications out o' birds flyin', stars fallin', bees hivin', and such. An' she'd lie awake — listenin' for calls, she said.'

'That don't prove naught,' said Tom. 'All Marsh folk has been smugglers since time ever-lastin'. 'Twould be in her blood to listen out o'nights.'

'Nature-ally,' old Hobden replied, smiling. 'I mind when there was smugglin' a sight nearer us than the Marsh be. But that wasn't my woman's trouble. 'Twas a passel o'no-sense talk,' he dropped his voice, 'about Pharisees.'

'Yes, I've heard Marsh men belief in 'em.' Tom looked straight at the wide-eyed children beside Bess.

'Pharisees,' cried Una. 'Fairies? Oh, I see!'

'People o' the Hills,' said the Bee Boy, throwing half of his potato towards the door.

'There you be!' said Hobden, pointing at him. 'My boy, he has her eyes and her out-gate senses. That's what she called 'em!'

'And what did you think of it all?'

'Um — um,' Hobden rumbled. 'A man that uses fields an' shaws after dark as much as I've done, he don't go out of his road excep' for keepers.'

'But settin' that aside?' said Tom, coaxingly. 'I saw ye throw the Good Piece out-at-doors just now. Do ye believe or — do ye?'

'There was a great black eye to that tater,' said Hobden, indignantly.

'My liddle eye didn't see un, then. It looked as if you meant it for — for Any One that might need it. But settin' that aside. D'ye believe or — do ye?'

'I ain't sayin' nothin', because I've heard naught, an' I've seen naught. But if you was to say there was more things after dark in the shaws than men, or fur, or feather, or fin, I dunno as I'd go far about to call you a liar. Now turnagain, Tom. What's your say?'

'I'm like you. I say nothin'. But I'll tell you a tale, an' you can fit it as how you please.'

'Passel o'no-sense stuff,' growled Hobden, but he filled his pipe.

'The Marsh men they call it Dymchurch Flit,' Tom went on slowly. 'Hap you have heard it?'

'My woman she've told it me scores o' times. Dunno as I didn't end by belieftin' it — sometimes.'

Hobden crossed over as he spoke, and sucked with his pipe at the yellow lanthorn flame. Tom rested one great elbow on one great knee, where he sat among the coal.

19

NEW ROMNEY

'Have you ever bin in the Marsh?' he said to Dan.

'Only as far as Rye, once,' Dan answered.

'Ah, that's but the edge. Back behind of her there's steeples settin' beside churches, an' wise women settin' beside their doors, an' the sea settin' above the land, an' ducks herdin' wild in the diks' (he meant ditches). 'The Marsh is justabout riddled with diks an' sluices, an' tide-gates, an' water-lets. You can hear 'em bubblin' an' grum-melin' when the tide works in 'em, an' then you hear the sea rangin' left and right-handed all up along the Wall. You've seen how flat she is – the Marsh? You'd think noth-in' easier than to walk eend-on acrost her? Ah, but the diks an' the water-lets, they twists the roads about as ravelly as witch-yarn on the spindles. So ye get all turned round in broad daylight.'

'That's because they've dreened the waters into the diks,' said Hobden. 'When I courted my woman the rushes was green – Eh me! the rushes was green – an' the Bailiff o' the Marshes, he rode up and down as free as the fog.'

'Who was he?' said Dan.

'Why, the Marsh fever an' ague. He's clapped me on the shoulder once or twice till I shook proper. But now the dreenin' off of the waters have done away with the fevers; so they make a joke, lik, that the Bailiff o' the Marshes broke his neck in a dik. A won'erful place for bees an' ducks 'tis too.'

'An' old,' Tom went on. 'Flesh an' Blood have been there since Time Everlastin' Beyond. Well, now, speakin' among themselves, the Marsh-men say that from Time Everlastin' Beyond, the Pharisees favoured the Marsh above the rest of Old England. I lay the Marsh men ought to know. They've been out after dark, father an' son, smugglin' some one thing or t'other, since ever wool grew to sheep's backs. They say there was always a middlin' few Pharisees to be seen on the Marsh. Impident as rabbits, they was. They'd dance on the nakid roads in the nakid daytime; they'd flash their liddle green lights along the diks, comin' an' goin', like honest smugglers. Yes, an' times they'd lock the church doors against parson an' clerk of Sundays.'

'That 'ud be smugglers layin' in the lace or the brandy till they could run it out o' the Marsh. I've told my woman so,' said Hobden.

'I'll lay she didn't belieft it, then – not if she was a Whit-gift. A won'erful choice place for Pharisees, the Marsh, by all accounts, till Queen Bess's father he come in with his Reformatories.'

Rudyard Kipling

THE 'PANTYLES'

At the foot of what is now called Frant Road, there used to flow a pretty little stream dividing the two counties of Kent and Sussex. The Chapel of Ease lay on the Kentish side, but was itself built across the boundary of two parishes – Speldhurst and Tonbridge. Thirty years ago, this Chapel had a most quaint appearance within. On the wall that stood in Speldhurst Parish was the old-fashioned 'three-decker' clerk's desk, reading desk, and pulpit, and on the opposite

THE PANTILES, TUNBRIDGE WELLS

side, under the great low gallery, was the communion table. The reason for this quaint arrangement was as follows: About 150 years ago, when the communion table was beneath the pulpit and reading desk, a certain rector of Speldhurst claimed the offertories of the Chapel. The then Incumbent was equal to the emergency! and transferring the Holy Table and its appurtenances across the Chapel into Tonbridge Parish, was able to snap his fingers at his adversary. The Chapel was skilfully restored later, and consecrated some two hundred years after the date it was built, by the Bishop of Dover.

On the Sussex side of the county stream – which now flows under the road and houses – were built the Assembly Rooms and the Theatre (now the Corn Exchange). A covered archway leads from the Frant Road to the Pantyles, passing the later building. At its entry there stood until four or five years ago, embedded in the ground, two small cannon, the remains of a little rank of artillery of five guns, which used to stand on a small grassy sward, close to the present railway tunnel, that passes under Frant Road. These guns were used for firing salutes in former days on the occasion of Royal visits to the Town.

The county stream before named soon became covered with houses where it flowed past the Pantyles, and many complications arose in consequence, connected with births, marriages and deaths. In recent times, cases have been known of this kind. On one occasion a death occurred in a room that happened to be over the County border, which necessitated a journey of eleven miles to Ticehurst, for the registry of the same. Another curious incident occurred in connection with a lodging house called 'The Coach and Horses', which, like most of the houses on one side of the Pantyles, was built over the County boundary. A poor tramp having died suddenly in this lodging house, an inquest was held in the room where the death occurred. A dispute having arisen, the County Surveyor was sent for, who with a piece of chalk, drew the County line across the floor. The boundary of the two counties passed beneath the tramp's bed; his head lay in Sussex, his body in Kent. The jury gave their verdict that a man's head was himself, and therefore the Sussex Parish was obliged to pay for his interment.

Lady Hope

21

THE MARRIAGE SERVICE

The Marriage Service itself used to be far more productive of scenes than it is now, and education is doing much to secure outward decorum, at any rate during the ceremony. Occasionally, however, still one's nerves are sorely taxed, by things said and done under the combined influence of nervousness, ignorance, and shyness. I did not argue much good from the preliminary questions of a 'hopper', who stopped me in the village street one Saturday evening after dark, and said –

'Please, sir, can you ask me twice one Sunday?' – meaning, I suppose, at morning and afternoon service both.

'No, friend,' I replied, 'I can't do that.'

Then, after a pause –

'Please, sir, can you marry me the same Sunday I'm asked out?' was his next inquiry.

I was obliged, of course, to say that I could not accommodate him even in this way.

'But,' I added, 'what makes you in such a hurry?'

'Well, you see sir,' he said, 'we're hoppers, and we don't want to be stopping about here after hops are done.'

I agreed to marry them at eight o'clock on the Monday morning after they were 'out-asked', and they accordingly presented themselves. All went well for a time, till suddenly the bridegroom put his head between his hands, began to cry, and walked away to the other end of the church. The bride did not look as much surprised as I should have expected, and the groomsman, another huge 'hopper', seemed barely surprised at all. Seeing, however, that his mate showed no signs of coming back, he turned half round, and called out with a loud voice –

'Come, Joe, be a man; stand up like a man, Joe.'

Upon this Joe slowly returned and stood up and said what was necessary. He went away again, but not till the essential part of the service was finished. After the service I asked the clerk what the meaning of this behaviour was. I though it must have been that the man was worse for drink but the explanation was that he had not long buried his first wife, and that he was overcome by his feelings.

John Coker Egerton

COAL MINING

But alas! as we are traversing, a mile or two further on, the long straight switchback road that heads across a sweep of open chalk country for Wingham, and can mark in the distance the woody hollow in which the townlet lies, a much less alluring object obtrudes itself upon the nearer vision. Now it ill becomes, perhaps, a resident of this Cinque-Port country, which has always paid more for its coal than any other part of England, to cavil at even a remote chance of some alleviation of the burden. Here, however, is one of a long line of some ten or a dozen mines spread at intervals of some distance across the Kent coal-fields. I am not qualified to make any statement as to their present condition or future possibilities, even if such were not beside the mark in these pages. Local rumour is busy enough with their affairs, but is no doubt mostly unreliable. Interest apparently centres in the quality of the coal rather than in the quantity, of which there is said to be any amount. Only a minority of these pits, I believe, have reached the producing

WINGHAM

EAST KENT COLLIERY, EYTHORNE

MAY DAY CELEBRATION

stage, the others having not yet got down deep enough. But I only set down what I have gathered up by the wayside, and no doubt the companies keep their secrets well, if they have any. I am told, and with something of the air of a grievance, that little or no local labour is employed even on the surface. All the miners are imported from the Black Country, mostly from Durham and North Lancashire, and no doubt they bring with them all those delightful amenities for which they are distinguished at home. I met a South Walian, however, one day upon the road, whistling 'Men of Harlech', which last patriotic display caused me to accost him and so confirm my suspicion of his nationality. They give one almost a shock when encountered in groups, these mannerless rather than unmannerly exotics upon the roads and lanes of rural Kent. One may wonder whether the mere atmosphere of this ancient civilization might in course of time smooth down some few of those fearsome angles that a semi-barbarous social demeanour and habit of life has caused to be cherished among them. When in their hours of copious leisure they fill the village alehouse, that time-honoured place of rustic rendezvous seems altogether at odds with the alien, harsh-throated crew. However, as they are here, and if the Kentish landscape is to be besmirched, let us hope they will some day provide us on the south-east coast with cheaper coal.

A.G. Bradley

MICROBES

The doctor was called in when absolutely needed, his medicine taken and thought highly of if it was nasty. Many household remedies were believed in. White oils were used for almost any pain; cobwebs (the dustier the better) were always used for cuts and to stop bleeding. Rue boiled in milk was thought very good for children in spring. Whitening and oil was a cure for burns, and it is very good, as I can testify.

The word 'microbe' had not been heard; infection was rather considered a fancy of the gentlefolks. Good mothers who knew how to manage, put all their children together when measles or whooping-cough appeared. In this way they 'got it over', to use their own words.

Whooping-cough was considered troublesome, but certain remedies for it were held in high estimation. Boiled onions, or onion gruel, was considered excellent. Butter and soft sugar made into a paste, others believed in. A red-hot poker in a bucket of pitch or tar which made a choking smoke was believed to be a perfect cure. Certainly children who were treated with it two or three times got well rapidly.

I wonder if the measured, weighed, inspected children of today will make the strong sensible men and women of the generation I am talking of!

Jane Connolly

24

THE DIALECT OF KENT

There is no such language as Anglo-Saxon; the very name is contradictory, for obviously one and the same language would not be spoken by two different, even though allied tribes. A better name would be Old English, but while the language of a country is a more or less unstable thing, and is, moreover, not universally spoken, it is better to give no names that suggest a common language for that country. The 'Anglo Saxon' or 'Old English' of the grammar books is generally Saxon – West Saxon – the language of Wessex. But even as there were three tribes that invaded these shores at the so-called Saxon Conquest – so there were three languages spoken. The Angles, who spread over the Midlands and the North, have left their name in East Anglia, and also the influence of the language. The Saxons did the same for the South – Wessex, Essex, Sussex, and so forth, and these two, the predominant partners as it were, have given their name to the resultant mixture of languages, even as they have done to the mixture of races.

But in Kent a third race settled – the Jutes – and they also have left their mark, which is chiefly to be found, however, in the remnants of the language that is still heard in the more remote parts of Kent, where the blight of the Cockney has not spread. The language is Jutish, becoming in the county 'Kentish', and Kentish has played no small part in our literary history, and many of the peculiarities of the spoken language of the county folk are not, as are often supposed, perversions of English, but rather the original language making a final struggle against extinction.

The earliest specimens of the dialect appear in various charters of the seventh and eighth centuries, but these are for the most part in Latin, only the place names being in Kentish. It is not till the ninth century that charters are found written wholly in the local dialect. Following these in date are a few sermons, *c.* 1250, to be found in the Bodleian library. They are translations, for a Kentish congregation, from some old French homilies, and are to be read in Morris's *Old English Miscellany*.

Half a century after these lived one of our most famous writers, William of Shoreham – a Kentish man by birth, who became afterwards vicar of Chart Sutton. He was one of the earliest translators of the Bible, and translated the Psalter, a copy of which, possibly in his writing, is in the British Museum Add. MSS 17376. The translation was in prose, but he was a poet of no mean order, and he wrote poems on various aspects of the Church teaching and ritual that are in places typical examples of Kentish, more so, perhaps, than his translation of the Psalms.

25

COOPERS

Another religious, Michel of Northgate, in Canterbury, a monk of Christ Church, also translated (1340) a French volume (*Le Soome des Vices et des Vertues*, written in 1279 by Frére Lorens (Laurentius Gallus) for Philip II of France) under the title of *The Remorse of Conscience (The Ayenbite of Inwyt)*. This deals with the Creed, the Commandments, holy living and dying, the deadly sins, the contrary virtues, and so forth, and is the finest specimen of the Kentish dialect that we possess, and together with some other fragments of the same date, and possibly by the same author, completes the total of the written examples of our Kentish dialect.

Frank C. Elliston-Erwood

KENTISH ALE

Faversham is an old rambling place with red-brick or half-timbered houses – mediaevally top-forward, many of them – and an old town hall with a neat cupola. It is a very ancient place, but best known because an Elizabethan wrote *Arden of Feversham* (so he spelt it), immortalising a murder sensation of his day. Faversham creek is navigable up to the town for vessels of two hundred tons. The town imports timber and coal,

exports hops and produce. The principal industry is oyster fishing. But let me not forget to mention that it brews excellent ale.

Drinks are never so good as in the places of their origin. It is a fact that in nearly all cases beers and wines that are to travel far have to be made differently from those that are to be consumed at home. I seldom – I must confess it – ask for Faversham Ale in foreign parts such as London and Dover, so do not know how far its flavour at home differs from what it is to strangers; but with lager outside Germany, Guinness outside Ireland, cider outside Devon or Brittany, and wines outside France, the Rhine, Italy, and (so far as I can hear) Australia, the case is notorious. The house-wife, I hear, has a prejudice against New Zealand mutton, and that never can be made in two qualities, one for export and one for New Zealand; far better founded must the prejudice be – so far as I can reason it out – against the drinks of foreign lands.

Each land, almost every county, has its own colours and atmosphere, as painters, doctors, naturalists, and agriculturists know. Kent to me is a land of red. The red Kentish Ale, the rich red of the conical tops surmounted by divergent funnels of the old oast-houses (as the hop-kilns are called) – different in colour from the cruder red of bricks made recently – the red-tiled roofs of villages beneath trees, red labels lettered with

THE TUDOR GATEWAY, ROCHESTER

'Rigden's Ales' at the top of inn walls, a red sail in a grey world with a line of green light on the sea below where a single bag of silver cloud shines out, red clay cliffs – these to me are Kentish notes. Kent is subjected to the English atmosphere and weathering power; its red is dulled to richness and mingled with other colour.

Arthur D. Lewis

OLD-DOORS

The door is a very important feature of the house, and tells of many happy comings and goings, and of some sad ones too. There the mother stands waiting to welcome her young children back from school. She is blest with many olive-branches, but a little later on she told me: 'When they are young they make your arms ache; when they are older they make your heart ache.' Poor mother! may that not be their common lot and experience. Through that door the labourer home returns weary with his daily toil saying to himself:

> Be the day weary, be the day long,
> At length it ringeth to evensong.

And great joy reigns when a soldier son from India enters through that door, and brings with him presents from that far-distant land, and tells his wondrous stories and adventures; or when a daughter who has married returns home for a holiday, bringing two tottering youngsters who are the pride and joy of their grand-parents.

The door and the threshold are very sacred. It is not well to stumble at the threshold, as Shakespeare, who knew his folk-lore, tells:

> For many men that stumble at the threshold
> Are well foretold that danger lurks within.

In olden days it was protected. A sacrifice was made when the threshold was laid. Amongst many peoples it was customary to sacrifice a calf or a sheep, or a hen, or a cock, and bury it beneath the stone in order to keep out evil spirits. The remains of animals so sacrificed have often been discovered beneath the thresholds of old houses. Witches used to be a great trouble to us, and we have scarcely yet ceased to believe in the power of the evil eye. Mysterious diseases carried off those who had incurred the wrath of a witch. Hence in order to prevent these old bel-dames from injuring us we still hang up horseshoes on our doors; but it is very important that the points should be upwards; otherwise they are of little use for keeping out witches. It will also be quite as effectual if we bury beneath the threshold bottles containing nails or pins. When a bride comes to her new home she should be carefully lifted over the threshold; otherwise ill-luck will befall her. Perhaps the cause of the custom of leaving open the door of a cottage may be traced to the traditional belief in the benevolent action of the good fairies, who used to perform all manner

SHEEP SHEARING

of kind actions for the housewife. They would churn the butter and do many other pleasant little 'odd jobs'. Certainly it was not an uncommon practice to leave a hole in the wall for the 'piskies', or pixies, to come in and out as they pleased.

Lest we become 'pixie-led', a dangerous form of letting one's wits go wool-gathering, let us look at the door itself. If it is old, it is probably made of oak and studded with nails, like one of the doors of the cottage at Small Hythe, near Tenterden. Sometimes there is a thumb-latch. The string-latch, which Red Riding-Hood was directed by the wolf to pull, has departed; but we stayed in an old abbey which has been restored by its present owner, who has introduced the string-latch for all the inner doors of his house; and it works admirably. At night many of these old doors were fastened by a heavy wooden bar passing across their whole length and fitting into holes in the walls of the house. Even the poor cottager was not always safe from midnight marauders and the lower ranks of highwaymen, and a good stout bar gave a sense of security.

P.H. Ditchfield

THE SHEEP OF THE MARSH

The Marsh has its mystery if you approach it properly, and most emphatically its beauty for those who love wide-open unencumbered plains, which sun gleams and cloud shadows touch so responsibly with flying feet. It has history, heaven knows, centuries of it, in which reckless lawbreakers, midnight rides, fierce encounters and the grim gallows-tree are the outstanding features. Above all these intangible attributes Romney Marsh has its sheep, and of that famous breed which has carried its name all over the world – thousands and thousands of them. A good-sized, white-faced sheep carrying an ample fleece, the 'Romney' or 'Kent' ought to be among the most profitable in the world, as unlike other heavy breeds its winter requirements are almost nil. On its own rich level pastures it has almost the hardy habit of a mountain sheep, which sounds paradoxical. Romney with its small sister marshes of Pevensey and the Stour on either side is the finest sheep land in Great Britain. The fact that much of it carries six to twelve big sheep to the acre will be sufficiently conclusive to the reader with the least pastoral knowledge, though it will not mean much to the artist. Nor anywhere can so many sheep be seen at a single

FAIRFOLD CHURCH

coup-d'oeil as from any height above the Marsh, particularly between Lydd and Rye, where there has been very little tillage. For elsewhere there is always a moderate acreage under the plough and there will almost certainly be more. But the wholesale breaking up of the finest old pasture land is not calculated to bring about the millennium of all-round productiveness that the Cockney who instructs the farmer through letters to the papers so ingenuously imagines. Unless, that is to say, half the industrial population of the towns are going to forsake them, a most improbable proposition, and turn market-gardeners, or small holders, for which they are less adapted by temperament, habit and tradition than probably any people in Europe.

The month of June, when the gleaming white of the freshly shorn sheep, which like ten thousand mushrooms dimple the radiant green of the early summer grass is the time to look down over the Marsh from some commanding height, such as Playden hill or even Rye town. I remember a prominent Scottish agriculturist, familiar with most of Great Britain, saying to me, when a hopeless invalid at the close of his life, that one of the things he always regretted having missed, was a sight of Romney Marsh in June, as there would be nothing like it, he thought, to the seeing eye, in the whole world – nor in all probability is there. An even distribution of some 150,000 sheep in so small an area is to be seen nowhere else. For those whom such things interest, it may be noted that all the lambs are removed from the Marsh in autumn to back-lying upland farms and brought back in April as tegs. This relieves the pressure when the grass is not growing and gives the young sheep a better chance to mature.

May is an anxious month on the Marsh with big sheep farmers, who have of course to stock up their pastures on the estimate of a normal season. If the rains hold off, as they occasionally do in this region of rather dry summers, for the very weeks when they are most wanted, the feebly growing young grasses get bitten down so close that they cannot properly respond to the refreshing showers when these eventually fall. The Romney Marsh sheep are sometimes crossed with the Southdown, but to nothing like the extent that crossing goes on nowadays in most parts of Britain. They have made great way too of late in South America and the Colonies, particularly in New Zealand, whose graziers come frequently back to the Marsh for breeding stock. The origin of the breed is lost in the mists of time, though a theory exists upon the Marsh that, owing to their amphibious qualities, Noah shipped a pair upon the Ark as more likely to survive the voyage than any other sort. The present type, however, seems little older than the last century, and the Leicester had no doubt something to do with improving and stereotyping it. But in early days cattle and pigs (the latter only as summer grazers before the mast in the upland woods) shared the Marsh with the sheep in relatively larger numbers than now. The polite palate professes a distaste for Romney Marsh mutton as too coarse, classing it with Lincoln, Leicester and the like. With the craze for small mutton and lamb which became universal in the 'eighties large mutton fell out of demand. The local gourmet, however, will tell you that Marsh mutton in the summer and autumn is the primest of meats. After all, these are salt marshes, and it is the mouton de pré-salé, that the Briton abroad welcomes or is expected to welcome on a table d'hôte menu. Furthermore all

THE LEES, FOLKESTONE

this mutton is grass-fed, and unlike other heavy breeds the fattening sheep get practically no turnips and not much cake at any time. They also lamb nearly as late as hill sheep, in April that is to say.

The farms upon the Marsh are large – five hundred, a thousand, even two thousand acres – though some are smaller. The land is curiously patchy, as one would expect from a country submerged within recorded history, but the better quality on the whole prevails, and that, whether in grass or in tillage, as are some parts where fine wheat is grown, is very good. In the great old days of the 'sixties and 'seventies £4 an acre was not an unusual rent, though it had been pushed up that high by competition beyond a doubt. About half, or less than half, that figure is the present standard, and I will undertake to say that in the tillage districts such hearing would make a visiting Lothian farmer's mouth water. A chronic theory of the Scottish farmer that the whole South is under-rented and enterprise thereby discouraged, would find here (in his eyes) an apotheosis of justification. But I shall get into trouble if I pursue so cryptic a subject any further. Most people are ready to tell the British farmer exactly what he ought to do, but few are interested in crops save vaguely as a feature in the landscape or as covert for partridges.

A.G. Bradley

OUT OF TOWN

Dickens wrote an article in praise of the Folkestone of yesterday and its big hotel – indeed, the article called 'Out of Town' referred to Folkestone as Pavilionstone, and declared 'The lion of Pavilionstone is its Great Hotel.' The whole article has a certain interest to students of modern history and change of manners and customs as chronicling the introduction of new standards of comfort into England.

A dozen years ago [it says], going over to Paris by South Eastern Tidal Steamer, you used to be dropped upon the platform of the main line Pavilionstone Station (not a junction then) at eleven o'clock on a dark winter's night, in a roaring wind; and in the howling wilderness outside the station, was a short omnibus which brought you up by the forehead the instant you got in at the door; and nobody cared about you and you were alone in the world. You bumped over infinite chalk, until you were turned out at a strange building which had just left off being a barn without having quite begun to be a house, where nobody expected your coming, or knew what to do with you when you were come, and where you were usually blown about, until you happened to be blown

FOLKESTONE HARBOUR

against the cold beef, and finally into bed. At five in the morning you were blown out of bed, and after a dreary breakfast, with crumpled company, in the midst of confusion, were hustled on board a steam-boat and lay wretched on deck until you saw France lunging and surging at you with great vehemence over the bowsprit.

Then follows an account of the advantages of the new Pavilionstone and its new Great Pavilionstone Hotel, where you find ready for you,

your news-room, dining-room, smoking-room, billiard-room, music-room, public breakfast, public dinner twice a day (one plain, one gorgeous), hot baths and cold baths. If you want to be bored, there are plenty of bores always ready for you, and from Saturday to Monday in particular, you can be bored (if you like it) through and through. Should you want to be private at our Great Pavilionstone Hotel, say but the word, look at the list of changes, choose your floor, name your figure . . .

A thoroughly good inn, in the days of coaching and posting, was a noble place. But no such inn would have been equal to the reception of four or five hundred people, all of them wet through and half of them dead sick, every day in the year. This is where we shine, in our Pavilionstone Hotel. Again – who, coming and going, pitching and tossing, boating and training, hurrying in

and flying out, could ever have calculated the fees to be paid at an old-fashioned house? In our Pavilionstone Hotel vocabulary, there is no such word as 'free'. Everything is done for you; every service is provided at a fixed and reasonable charge; all the prices are hung up in all the rooms; and you can make out your own bill beforehand, as well as the book-keeper.

Thus does Dickens speak of the change in comfort during his day. By all accounts, a similar change has gone on during the time of any middle-aged man of today. What was luxury forty years ago is a sufficiency today. The distance in habit and income between class and class gets steadily greater . . .

Arthur D. Lewis

OLD SAYINGS

I have frequently heard the following sayings: 'Cobham Churchyard's full of Savages;' 'Northfleet Churchyard's full of Badgers,' 'Meopham Churchyard's full of Buggs.'

The 'Savages,' 'Badgers', and 'Buggs' are the names of some of the old families lying in the churchyards mentioned. These surnames, I believe, are still to be found in their respective parishes.

Geo. Smith

HEVER CASTLE

HOPELESS DIRECTIONS

Edenbridge Station is about a mile from the village. The church is small, but it gives that air of dignity and peace to the scene which is so seldom absent in rural England. 'The walk to Hever,' says the *Handbook*, 'across the fields from Edenbridge, is a pleasant one.' This was quite enough to set me hunting diligently for it. Most of the townsfolk declared they had never heard of such a walk, and looked upon me with manifest coldness and suspicion, as if I were a sort of cross between a tramp and a policeman. One man told me to go through the churchyard and then go 'straight forrards'. I went 'forrards' until I found myself brought up at a five-barred gate, without track of any kind leading from it. Then I turned back to get fresh directions. An old woman now appeared, and said you could go by the fields to Hever Castle, leastways if the paths were not stopped up; but no stranger could find the way. She told me how to go, but unfortunately her directions were far more hopelessly entangled than those which the clown gives to the footsore stranger in the pantomime. I therefore gave up the field path, and took with reluctance to the turnpike road. There is not much to be said for this road, except that it is tolerably short — the distance to the castle being three miles. About half-way I met with a brother tramp — a man of foreign appearance, very thin and poor, with something tied up in a torn and dirty pocket-handkerchief, and limping slowly and painfully along. He said nothing, and I passed on; but presently the man's starved look and wan face smote upon me, and I looked back. He was hobbling on at the rate of about

half a mile an hour. I leaned over a gate and waited till he came up.

'You seem tired,' said I, 'suppose you take this towards your night's lodging,' and I offered him sixpence.

'I didn't ask for anything, did I?' replied he with a frightened look.

'No, but take it all the same.'

'I don't want it — not but what I'm poor enough God knows.'

'Well then, why not have this trifle?'

'I have just come out of prison for begging a penny on the road, and now you are offering me this to get me another month — I didn't ask you for anything, did I? Keep your money.'

This, upon the whole, is the most wonderful occurrence that has happened to me in all my walks. My thirsty fellow-tramps have generally taken my small contributions in the most obliging manner.

I soon left this poor fellow far behind, and came to Hever Castle — the castle to which Mr Froude's hero, Henry the Eighth, went a-courting to Anne Boleyn. I saw the moat, and the pleasant gardens round about it, and the red and white roses which have been trained to grow up each side of the principal entrance — but more than that I was not allowed to see. 'Master says as no strangers can come in,' said the servant-girl. Whereupon I took myself off. But at the church I was more successful, thanks to the schoolmaster, who keeps the keys. There are two fine brasses in this poor, neglected, dilapidated church — one to the father of Anne Boleyn, in perfect

THE TOWN HALL, FORDWICH

condition, and dated 1538. The other is to the memory of Margaret Cheyne, dated 1419. 'Your church is in a shocking state,' said I to the schoolmaster.

'Yes, sir,' he said, 'we have no resident gentry now about here, and no one will do anything for it.' The pews are evidently ancient, and there is an old oaken staircase, quite rough, going up the tower to the clock. But the damp is cracking the walls in all directions, and it may be doubted whether the tower itself – a picturesque object for miles around – will last very many years longer if something is not done to strengthen it.

'The Rector,' remarked the schoolmaster, 'thinks of appealing to the public for help – we are all very poor about here. It is a dreadfully poor place.'

I hope the Rector will succeed, for otherwise the old church will come tumbling about his ears one of these days.

Louis J. Jennings

DUCKING A 'WITCH'

The old governing body of Fordwich could lawfully inflict capital punishment and the spot where the sentence of death was carried out was known as the Feswelle, or Thieves' Well. Malefactors condemned to death, after being bound, were put to death by the prosecutor, whose duty it was to do as is done

with surplus kittens – hold their heads under water until they were dead. The well was long ago filled up and the only traces of it left are some stones in the wall of a cottage garden lying between the church and the infants' school. It is strange how the mode of capital punishment varied in the various Cinque Ports. At Dover, for instance, the culprit was thrown over Sharpness Cliff, and at Sandwich the poor wretches were buried alive in Thieves' Down.

An incident which caused amusement at the time, although it might have been fraught with a tragic result, occurred not long ago, when a party of excursionists rigged up the ducking stool and began the process of dipping. All went swimmingly; but they wished to see the experiment more practically demonstrated, and a small boy standing near readily volunteered to impersonate the 'witch' for the sake of a copper. He was straightway fastened in the chair the pulley was left go and down he went to the bottom of the river. But then, when it was attempted to pull him up again the rope would not work. They pulled, they tugged, they yelled, but no, the rope was twisted and would not budge an inch. And all this time the unhappy small boy was being steadily drowned like a rat in a trap. At last, oh great relief! the rope moved, the chair came up with a bound and the senseless victim was hauled out more dead than alive. No ill effects followed his voluntary ducking, but no one has had the temerity to dip a witch since.

Charles Igglesden

33

MASTER KELLY, FRUITERER

MAIDSTONE COUNTY COURT

John Leney, Maidstone, v. Thomas Reeves, Maidstone. – Defendant is a greengrocer in Stone-street, and the plaintiff lives in Knightrider-street, the claim (18s.) being for injury to plaintiff's son through his being run over by the defendant. Mrs Leney said she had to pay a doctor's bill amounting to 10s. 6d. and she lost a week's work in consequence of having to attend to the child. James Austen said he was at work in Knightrider-street, when he thought he heard a horse running away. He saw a horse coming along 'like steam', and the defendant could not hold it. He was on the wrong side of the road, and witness saw him run over the little boy. He also saw him hit the horse two or three times. Defendant now stated that he was not driving fast or carelessly. The child ran out of a passage, and did not look to see if there was a cart coming. Witness pulled to the other side of the road to avoid running over him, but he ran into the road. He might have been driving five miles an hour. For the defence, John White said he met the defendant with his trap in Knightrider-street, and he saw the child run into the road. Defendant tried to pull the horse to the off side, and the child stopped in the centre of the road. The horse appeared to become startled and started off. Defendant was not driving at more than the rate of five or six miles an hour. James Austen: He was going ten miles an hour. Defendant consented to pay the doctor's bill, amounting to 10s. 6d. His Honour said he was inclined to think that the defendant was not to blame.

The Maidstone and Kent County Standard

WINTER LANDSCAPE

SOME CURIOUS OLD CUSTOMS IN EAST KENT

As we sit around the blazing log fire on a winter's evening, it is a most interesting pastime to recount the various customs observed and fancies cherished by the rustics in 'the good old days'. The spread of education has done much to banish ostensible superstition, but popular beliefs and customs are not easily eradicated. Though discredited, they die hard – die a lingering death, so chronic that one hesitates to speak of an old custom or habit as a thing of the past, lest it should be discovered later in some remote corner of our County.

The belief still survives that, on Christmas Eve, exactly at the hour of midnight, a certain rose slowly opens and re-closes its petals to salute the birthday of our Lord; and some of the old country folk also believe that, at the same moment, and for the same purpose, all the sheep in the meadows turn and bow towards the East.

Of those old customs which have come down to us, either by record or observation, some may be relics of the Druidical period, whilst others are obviously no older than the dark ages when Romanism went stalking to and fro in our land.

A favourite practice among farm-hands, on Christmas Eve, was to go A Hodening – a custom that varied a trifle in different districts. A full-sized horse's head was carved in wood, and hollowed, with two large round holes made for the eyes. The lower jaw was hung on hinges, and supported by a rope passed round a sheave inside the head, by which it could be closed. Some large-headed iron nails were driven into both jaws to form the teeth. The head was then fixed to a short pole, about four feet long, and carried by the strongest of the company, known as 'the horse'. He had to stoop to make as good a 'back' as possible, supporting himself by the pole. Over him was spread a horse-cloth, and one of the smaller lads mounted to be the 'jockey'. Another member of the party, called 'the old woman', was dressed in female clothing, and carried a broom. Of the remainder (all of whom were fantastically attired) the two strongest were told off for defence in case of molestation, and the others sang carols. Frequently they would also carry handbells, and burn a candle in the 'horse's head', for the light to shine through like a turnip lantern.

When all was ready, the company sallied forth in their wonderful array to make calls upon some of the better-class residents. On arriving at a house, one of them would knock, and the others rang their bells. As the door opened, 'the old woman' began sweeping the feet of the person who appeared, while 'the horse' pranced and snorted, and gnashed his teeth. The awful din can be imagined better than described. If the inmates accorded them a welcome – generally by gifts of ale and cake, or of money – the carollers proceeded with their melodies.

In course of time it became too boisterous for the improved tastes of the bourgeoisie. Fresh troupes sprang up, having no connection with farms, and neither knowing nor caring anything about the tradition of the custom. Irregularities were introduced until, as they say in local parlance, 'it went on anyhow, like Rainham fair.'

MARGATE

The magistrates in the Isle of Thanet suppressed this custom about fifty or sixty years ago, when a woman at Broadstairs was so terrified by the hodening-horse that she died of fright; but it continued to be observed for some time afterwards outside the pale of their jurisdiction.

Originally, real horses' heads appear to have been used, but as they were not always procurable wooden ones became regular substitutes. In like manner, the horse-cloth had succeeded an animal's skin.

Masquerading in 'fancy dress' used to be exceedingly popular in East Kent, on dark evenings, particularly at Christmas time, although the sport was also indulged in on Guy Fawkes' Day. It has been stated that a woman was frightened to death, early in the last century, through meeting a man dressed as a bear; but that may be only another version of the incident mentioned above. A relative of the writer, when walking home along a dark lane near Faversham, on a fifth of November night, encountered a man disguised as 'Satan', and held him by his tail until he revealed his identity. The wearing of skins of cattle and carrying heads of animals seems to have been a very old custom in this part, possibly dating from the time of the ancient Britons. It was condemned by Archbishop Theodore, at about the year 680, after which artificial heads and skins were generally adopted.

The fishermen of Folkestone had a Christmas custom of their own. Eight of the largest and best whitings would be selected from the catch whenever a smack returned. These fish, known as 'rumball whitings', would be sold separately, and the money kept for providing a feast on Christmas Eve, which they called a Rumball. The skipper of each smack managed the feast for his crew and their friends, so there was the same number of feasts as there were boats. The custom seems to have fallen into desuetude about a century ago, but long afterwards Christmas Eve continued to be known as 'rumball night', and was set apart for social festivities. It has been suggested that the feast was originally instituted in honour of St Rumbald or Rumwold, whose protection of the fishery it was desired to obtain.

Probably before this number of the *Invicta* has been long in the hands of its numerous readers, they will be reminded of the festive season by the 'waits' disturbing the otherwise quiet hours of night, and by that other custom, not confined to East Kent, that seems to have risen rapidly in the esteem of the poorer youngsters in our towns. Two or three boys (the girls seem to enjoy it as well), without any particular costumes, except rags, make a tour of the larger houses, and after ringing the bell or rattling the knocker, recite:

> Christmas is coming, the turkeys are fat;
> Please drop a penny in a poor boy's hat;
> If ye havn't a penny, a ha'p'ny will do:
> If ye havn't a ha'p'ny – then God bless you!

Amen.

Sidney Bredgar

'ARRY AND 'ARRIET

In a book like this, which, as its title no doubt suggests, is mainly concerned with things of the past, it would be out of order to dwell at any length on these large watering-places

CRICKET WEEK, TUNBRIDGE WELLS

which have in recent times grown out of the old Cinque-Ports and their limbs. Still their early rise and growth is closely linked with the changes in our national life and goes back into days that we are accustomed to regard as having much of the glamour of the past, if not of a past quite in the Cinque-Port sense. Particularly in this case with those that are no longer regarded by the fastidious as eligible, that have long ago lost any pretension, even in advertisements, to being 'select' and are frankly the resort of the multitude. Eastbourne and Bournemouth are, no doubt, ornate and select, but they have no story and no past. But when one reads letters written a hundred and fifty years ago from some fashionable dame, extolling Margate as the very cream of *bon ton*, or from a gentleman 'of very respectable family', enumerating with ingenuous vanity the 'persons of quality' with whom he has rubbed shoulders at Ramsgate, one begins to feel that these places have a peculiar social history of their own and a past with its own particular appeal. And it is in the older and shabbier terraces where 'Arry and 'Arriet are most in evidence at their shrimps and tea. One may picture, if one chooses, the be-wigged and many-waistcoated beaux ogling the self-conscious belles as they minced past the windows on their way to hear the latest gossip at the subscription rooms, or to face the dreadful joys of the new bathing machines.

A.G. Bradley

CRICKET

Cricket is, of course, our favourite summer game, though it rarely flourishes in any parish in which there is not some resident gentleman who, being himself fond of it, gives it his personal encouragement. It would seem that in times past our county produced players who were as giants to their degenerate successors. At one of our village matches I remember happening to say that the man then batting was having a good innings. This harmless remark was at once rebuked by a reference to days gone by.

'Ah, well!' said an old man, 'it ain't nothin' to an innings I mind a man havin' at "The Wells" [Tunbridge Wells] time as I used to go carrier to "The Borough" – he was in three days, he was, and never was out.'

I signified my admiration.

'Yes,' added the man, 'I know it was three days, for I mind he was in when I went by with the broad wheel wagon to London, and he was in when I came back.'

It was a single-wicket match, it is true – so the man said; still, my recollections pale before his. This statement has been verified to me. The match was between Mr Thomas Foster, of Penshurst, and Mr W. Richardson, of Leigh, on the one side, and two well-known players, Messrs Cooper and Driver, on the other. It was played on Southborough Common near Tunbridge Wells, in some year between 1816 and 1820. A nephew

37

'A PONDEROUS LOCOMOTIVE ENGINE'

of Mr Foster, the hero of the three days' innings, has kindly sent me this corroboration of the remark which I casually heard on our cricket-ground.

John Coker Egerton

BIDDENDEN

A correspondent writes: On Saturday evening last, owing to unskilful steering, a ponderous locomotive engine, belonging to Messrs Knight, of Sittingbourne, and dragging six large trucks laden with sixteen tons of wool, got off the main road leading to Headcorn just outside the village of Biddenden, and sank up to its firebox in the soft turfy siding of the road, close to the water-table. Considering the unceasing torrents of rain that fell throughout the whole day, such leviathan engines, drawing such heavy loads, can scarcely be considered fair usage of the highways of the Weald of Kent.

The Maidstone and Kent County Standard

BABY FOLK-LORE

During a conversation with a Kentish woman (a native of Greenhithe), the other day, I gathered the following pieces of folk-lore respecting babies:

If babies are made to look at themselves in a looking-glass, before they are a twelve-month old, they will 'cut their teeth crosswise'.

If the feet of a baby be tickled it will make the young 'toddlekin' stutter.

If the finger nails of an infant be cut before it is a year old, it will develop a light-fingered tendency in after life.

These beliefs, no doubt, have their counterparts in other counties; indeed, the 'nail-cutting' superstition seems to be a widely-spread one. In some parts of Sussex it appears the fingernails of baby must not be cut at all – they should be bitten off to prevent the child growing up dishonest. In Kent (and probably elsewhere) they say, 'people who bite their fingernails are falsehood tellers.'

McB

OUTSIDE ST BART'S ALMSHOUSES

SCYTHING

WILLIAM SUTTON

FARMING INTERESTS

During the year 1886 the farming interest all over Kent and Sussex expressed its indignation at the unfairness of the extraordinary tithe, and the agitation reached such a height that in the village of Biddenden, a sensational riot occurred. The scene was at Wagstaff Farm, the occupier being Mr W. Weekes, and on behalf of the Rev. W. Peterson, the rector of Biddenden, a distress sale was announced to take place. The crowd that had gathered was aroused to such a state of indignation that the auctioneer was roughly handled, and in the end Mr Weekes and Mr Gower, of Biddenden, and Messrs G. Cooper, W. Gillet, C. Batt and D. Batt of Smarden, were brought before the magistrates at Cranbrook. Cooper was sentenced to a month's imprisonment with hard labour and the rest fined £5 each. If the excitement over the distress sale had been great, the consternation knew no bounds, when the agitators found one of their number sent to prison like a common felon. Meetings were held and a petition, containing seventeen hundred and sixty-six signatures, was forwarded to the Home Secretary, and as a result the sentence was reduced by one week. Although many would attach blame to the Biddenden agitators, there was no disguising the fact that the riot at Wagstaff Farm brought about immediate legislation on the subject, and in the year 1886 an Act was passed providing that the extraordinary tithe, which was chargeable upon hop, fruit and market garden grounds, should not be levied on land brought under such cultivation after the passing of the Act. The following description of the scene at Wagstaff Farm, which appeared in the *Kentish Express* of February 27th, 1886 will be read with interest.

Police-Sergeants Harmer and Fowle were on the ground with a posse of nine policemen. Mr Byrne, of the firm of Pettit, Son and Byrne, Goldersquare, London, was the auctioneer. This gentleman proceeded from the house to a field in front, where it was intended to hold the sale. His appearance was the signal for a number of jeering remarks, and he walked on amidst a knot of anything but admirers to a couple of waggons, into one of which he, together with several other people, mounted and proceeded to open the sale, handing forth bills. Whilst so engaged there was a shout of 'Run him in the pond.' This remark, meeting with the approval of the majority present, was put into practice, a large number catching hold of the waggon and running it down the field towards the pond, into which the waggon was forced. Fortunately the pond was very shallow, the wheels only going about a foot deep in mud and water; the occupants of the waggon being the auctioneer, Mr Weekes, and a reporter. After a deal of bantering on the part of the company, the waggon was pulled out and run a short distance up the field, to be only once more run at a trot down a short bank into the middle of the pond, amid cries of 'Turn the waggon over' and 'Take the shafts off and leave him in.' At this time the auctioneer and reporter had the interior of the waggon all to themselves. The waggon was once more pulled out and ran up the field towards a pool of larger size and a depth of about nine feet, but ere the procession had, amidst peals of laughter, jeering and shouting, reached the middle of the field, the auctioneer got out of the waggon and was immediately pounced upon by the people. Then commenced a regular struggle between Mr Weekes and the police on one hand with the people on the other for the body of the unfortunate auctioneer. The struggling was enlivened by the casual throwing of rotten eggs, which amusement proved far more odorous than pleasant to several in the crowd. Several times the auctioneer was collared and taken possession of by the crowd only to be again rescued from rough horse-play by the police. The auctioneer and escort made their way, struggling as before, to Mr Weekes's house, only to find the front door locked against them. This caused roars of laughter from the company, who seemed thoroughly to enjoy the fun of impeding the progress of the sale. Whilst standing at the front door an upstairs window was opened and a piece of cocoa-nut matting was let fall on the auctioneer and escort. This matting was thrown amongst the crowd, some of whom quickly dipped it in a tub of water and again threw it at Mr Byrne. There happened to be a slit in the matting, and, unfortunately for the victim, the matting fell in such a way that his head, which was bare, went through the hole, the dirty, muddy and wet matting hanging on him like a large apron. This sorry spectacle increased, if possible, the mirth of the crowd, which was overwhelming, when some of the womenfolk from the same window threw basins of cold water upon the already much-dejected gentleman. Someone in the crowd threw a lighted squib amongst the police, one of the policemen's clothing being burnt by it. The police also received, as did Mr Weekes, a good quantity of water

SUNDAY MORNING, CHATHAM BARRACKS

from the windows, but they bore it unruffled, and throughout the scrimmage kept their tempers remarkably well. A rush was then made to get round the side of the house, which, however, was at first unsuccessful, and, notwithstanding the clamour, the auctioneer again attempted to carry out his duties, whereupon a bid was made for the first lot, including 27 ewe tegs, and they were bought in for Mr Weekes for £44. Another rush was made for the back door of the house, which was also found to be locked. A dispute here arose as to the legality of the posters announcing the sale, which still further increased the hub-bub. Someone cried out, 'Will you come down here to another sale?' To this Mr Byrne replied that he should not. This caused another shout of 'Give us a crown for the Association.' This was replied to by Mr Weekes calling out that Mr Byrne promised to give 5s. and not come again. Mr Weekes continuing, said, 'You are as safe as the Bank of England now, and you are now converted into a good man.' This statement was received with vociferous cheering for the auctioneer, and he having been taken into the farmhouse, the crowd went across the field to hold an indignation meeting.

Thus ended one of the most remarkable scenes in the Weald of Kent.

Charles Igglesden

GAD'S HILL RUSTIC SPORTS

In this letter to Macready (of 28 December 1866), the novelist gives an account of some races and other festivities which he had organized, and which had taken place two days previously.

You will be interested in knowing that, encouraged by the success of summer cricket-matches, I got up a quantity of foot-races and rustic sports in my field here on the twenty-sixth last past: as I have never yet had a case of drunkenness, the landlord of the Falstaff had a drinking-booth on the ground. All the prizes I gave were in money, too. We had two thousand people here. Among the crowd were soldiers, navvies, and labourers of all kinds. Not a stake was pulled up, or a rope slackened, or one farthing's-worth of damage done. To every competitor (only) a printed bill of general rules was given, with the concluding words: 'Mr Dickens puts every man upon his honour to assist in preserving order.' There was not a dispute all day, and they went away at sunset rending the air with cheers, and leaving every flag on a six-hundred yards' course as neat as they found it when the gates were opened at ten in the morning. Surely this is a bright sign in the neighbourhood of such a place as Chatham!

Frederic G. Kitton.

TOAD ROCK

ROCKS

On Rusthall Common is the famous Toad Rock, which is to Tunbridge Wells what Thorwaldsen's lion is to Lucerne, and the Leaning Tower to Pisa. Lucerne's lion emerged from the stone under the sculptor's mallet and chisel, but the Rusthall monster was evolved by natural processes, and it is a toad only by courtesy. An inland rock is, however, to most English people so rare an object that Rusthall has almost as many pilgrims as Stonehenge. The Toad is free; the High Rocks, however, which are a mile distant, cannot be inspected by the curious for less than sixpence. One must pass through a turnstile before these wonders are accessible. Rocks in themselves have insufficient drawing power, as the dramatic critics say, a maze has been added, together with swings, a seesaw, arbours, a croquet lawn, and all the proper adjuncts of a natural phenomenon. The effect is to make the rocks appear more unreal than any rocks ever seen upon the stage.

E. V. Lucas

FIRST LOVE

As the year slid through the fogs into the spring, he persuaded Joanna to come with him on his rambles on the Marsh. He was astonished to find how little she knew of her own country, of that dim flat land which was once under the sea. She knew it only as the hunting ground of her importance. It was at Yokes Court that she bought her roots, and from Becket's House her looker had come; Lydd and Rye and Romney were only market towns – you did best in cattle at Rye, but the other two were proper for sheep; Old Honeychild was just a farm where she had bought some good spades and dibbles at an auction; at Misleham they had once had foot-and-mouth disease – she had gone to Picknye Bush for the character of Milly Pump, her chicken-girl . . .

He told her of the smugglers and owlers who had used the Woolpack as their headquarters long ago, riding by moonlight to the cross-roads, with their mouths full of slang – cant talk of 'mackerel' and 'fencing' and 'hornies' and 'Oliver's glim'.

43

CHURCH INTERIOR AT IVYCHURCH

'Well, if they talked worse there then than they talk now, they must have talked very bad indeed,' was all Joanna found to say.

He told her of the old monks of Canterbury who had covered the Marsh with the altars of Thomas à Becket.

'We got shut of 'em all on the fifth of November,' said Joanna, 'as we sing around here on bonfire nights – and "A halfpenny loaf to feed the Pope, a penn'orth of cheese to choke him," as we say.'

All the same he enjoyed the expeditions that they had together in her trap, driving out on some windy-skied March day, to fill the hours snatched from her activities at Ansdore and his muddlings at North Farthing, with all the sea-green sunny breadth of Walland, and still more divinely with Walland's secret places – the shelter of tall reeds by the Yokes Sewer, or of a thorn thicket making a tent of white blossom and spindled shadows in the midst of the open land.

Sometimes they crossed the Rhee Wall on to Romney Marsh, and he showed her the great church at Ivychurch, which could have swallowed up in its nave the two small farms that make the village. He took her into the church at New Romney and showed her the marks of the Great Flood, discolouring the pillars for four feet from the ground.

'Doesn't it thrill you? – Doesn't it excite you?' he teased her, as they stood together in the nave, the church smelling faintly of hearthstones.

'How long ago did it happen?'

'In the year of our Lord twelve hundred and eighty-seven the Kentish river changed his mouth, and after swilling out Romney Sands and drowning all the marsh from Honeychild to the Wicks, did make himself a new mouth in Rye Bay, with which mouth he swallowed the fifty taverns and twelve churches of Broomhill, and – '

'Oh, have done talking that silly way – it's like the Bible, only there's no good in it.'

Her red mouth was close to his in the shadows of the church – he kissed it . . .

'Child!'

'Oh, Martin – '

She was faintly shocked because he had kissed her in church, so he drew her to him, tilting back her chin.

'You mustn't' . . . but she had lost the power of gainsaying him now, and made no effort to release herself. He held her up against the pillar and gave her mouth another idolatrous kiss before he let her go.

'It all happened that while back, they might at least have got the marks off by this time,' she said, tucking away her loosened hair.

Martin laughed aloud – her little reactions of common sense after their passionate moments never failed to amuse and delight him.

'You'd have had it off with your broom, and that's all you think about it. But look here, child – what if it happened again?'

'It can't.'

HIGH STREET, TUNBRIDGE WELLS

'How do you know?'

'It can't. I know it.'

'But if it happened then it could happen again.'

'There ain't been a flood on the Marsh in my day, nor in my poor father's day, neither. Sometimes in February the White Kemp brims a bit, but I've never known the roads covered. You're full of old tales. And now let's go out, for laughing and love-making ain't the way to behave in church.'

'The best way to behave in church is to get married.'

She blushed faintly and her eyes filled with tears.

Sheila Kaye-Smith

AN ANCIENT MARRIAGE CUSTOM

In the olden time, when a couple in Kent became 'engaged', it was the custom for the bethrothal to be made in the church of the parish where one of the contracting parties resided, and then the first part of the marriage service was read. Consequently, only the remaining portion was used at the wedding. There appears to have been no specified period between the two ceremonies, which occasionally extended into a few years – and it is quite possible that sometimes the second event never came off.

The Invicta Magazine Vol. 1

POVERTY

On introducing myself to the secretary of the Manchester Town Mission, Mr Geldart, I mentioned to him that I was surprised to find, that wherever the aristocracy, squirearchy, and gentry were congregated together, there the moral, social, and physical condition of the people was lower and more frightful than in the manufacturing towns. He said, 'You are quite right in the conclusion you have come to, but you are not the first to make the discovery. I published,' said he, 'more than twenty years since, a paper containing statistical information which left no doubt upon the subject and the town from which I took my data was Tunbridge Wells.' He continued, 'My statements at that time were universally disbelieved, and were regarded as having proceeded from an over-heated brain and an inaccurate head, rather than from the pen of a sober and prudent calculator. The truth, however,' said he, 'must at last prevail and come to light, notwithstanding all the malice, effort, and opposition of men to strangle it, and keep it in the dark.'

I was anxious, after hearing this statement, to become personally acquainted with Tunbridge Wells; and although I did not expect to find it in the condition described by Mr Geldart more than twenty years since, still I felt interested in paying it a visit. I arrived there on the Friday, and went to visit one of the missionaries, who informed me that the morrow was their holiday on which day he declined working with me. I was

THE PANTILES, TUNBRIDGE WELLS

leaving on the Monday, consequently, had no alternative but to go alone. The missionary named to me the parts most desirable to see, and provided me with a number of tracts, in order to enable me to enter the place in *propria persona*, to try my hand for the first time as an amateur missionary. I commenced in Gas Lane, a low district, which I had considerable difficulty in finding, as it is so situated as to be almost cut off from the other parts of the town; and when in it, it seemed as if I was quite alone in my new vocation. Had the people been inclined for pocket picking, or taking forcible possession of my person, no obstacle stood in the way to prevent them. There were no passengers, except those who were there located; no carts, carriages, wagons, wheelbarrows, or costermongers, or any other vehicle, that gave indications of street business being carried on – nothing that resembled the traffic of a town. I approached a man standing outside his house, smoking his pipe, who stared at me as if I had been the beadle of the parish, or the Lord Mayor going to the Mansion House, pondering, no doubt, in his mind, who I could be, what I could want, and what was about to happen to the inhabitants of Gas Lane, Tunbridge Wells. I wished him good morning, to which he replied very civilly. I then began a short disputation on smoking, which engaged his attention, so far as to ensure me an acceptance. I stated that smoking was all very well in moderation, but when indulged in to excess, was calculated to injure the health; in this he perfectly agreed. Finding myself now on pretty good terms with him, I proceeded to business by asking him if he ever went to church. Here I had to learn a lesson in my new vocation.

'Church!' said he; 'why, is not reading the Bible at home as good as going to church?' He then said, 'Why won't the chapel do as well as the church?' Most likely he took me for a stray parson, and for that reason objected to the church.

I replied, 'If you read your Bible at home, and act up to the principles therein contained, and lead a life which brings peace to your hearth, by doing your duty to God, yourself, and your neighbours, I am the last man in the world to enforce your going to church, although I believe you would nevertheless be all the better, and none the worse for so doing.' This seemed reasonable, and the impression made upon him was decidedly favourable. I then continued, 'As to the chapel, go there if you like; one place is just as good as another.' We were now good friends. This conversation brought out others to listen to the stranger. This gave me the opportunity of delivering them a tract each. I had now established myself in their good graces, by proving to them that I did not come there as a representative of any particular church. It was a decided success upon the principle of non-sectarian doctrine.

And this is the means by which the town missionaries of England have succeeded in making, not only a good, but a deep impression upon the minds of many, so as ultimately to be an instrument in the hands of God of turning many a sinner from his course of wickedness, and making him an heir of glory. I had now so far ingratiated myself with them, that on leaving, they said, 'Well sir, when are you coming to see us again?'

THE COMMON, TUNBRIDGE WELLS

I said 'Most probably never; I am a visitor, making a short stay in the town – but should I return, it would give me great pleasure to come and see you again.' I wished them good morning, telling them they had my best wishes for their temporal and eternal welfare.

Wishing to see something of the interior of their dwellings, I knocked at a door, and begged most respectfully to be admitted, by saying, 'Good morning to you! how do you do? Will you allow me to come in and have a chat with you. I am a stranger here.' A rough mannered woman, slamming the door in my face, said,

'I shall not, I don't know anything about you.'

This was putting the extinguisher upon the candle most effectually. I was regularly *non plussed*. Nothing daunted by the severe rebuff, I resolved to make the attempt a second time. Seeing three or four women sauntering about the doorway, some in, and others out, I approached them most civilly, and saying, 'Will you allow me to come in and say a word to you?'

'No!' said the mistress, 'I shall not.' I thanked her for her incivility with a polite bow, and walked about my business perfectly content with my lot, not at all ruffled at the want of sympathy, pondering over some of the difficulties the poor town and city missionaries have to contend with. I at last succeeded in getting the *entrée* to a house by knocking at a door,

when a poor woman gave me a most welcome and polite reception. She was a Christian, and in deep poverty too. The poor woman told me part of her woe with an affability and frankness of manner, as if I had known her for twenty years. She said, she had once been well off in the world, and had kept a small shop, but could not stoop to some of the dirty tricks of trade without sacrificing her Christian principles, and had to contend with other shops, as rivals, quite near at hand, added to which, some unfortunate customers did not pay her what they owed, and thus sent her to the wall. The poor woman was almost broken-hearted. We met as perfect strangers – we parted friends. I shook her cordially by the hand, told her to cheer up, to put her trust in God, in whom she would find a friend that would stick closer to her than a brother. The missionary who supplied me with tracts informed me that, seven years since, not even a policeman would have dared to pass down Gas Lane by himself. So much for missionary influence at Tunbridge Wells.

After this, I repaired to a part of the town near to the Jolly Sailors where I was kindly received in several houses, and only met with one rebuff or refusal to step over the threshold; and thus ended my visit to Tunbridge Wells.

J. Shaw

CHERRY PICKERS

THE CHERRY PICKERS

Three fruit-pickers – women – were the first people I met near the village (in Kent). They were clad in 'rags and jags', and the face of the eldest was in 'jags' also. It was torn and scarred by time and weather; wrinkled, and in a manner twisted like the fantastic turn of a gnarled tree-trunk, hollow and decayed. Through these jags and tearings of weather, wind, and work, the nakedness of the countenance – the barren framework – was visible; the upper-lip smooth, and without the short groove which should appear between lip and nostrils. Black shadows dwelt in the hollows of the cheeks and temples, and there was a blackness about the eyes. This blackness gathers in the faces of the old who have been much exposed to the sun, the fibres of the skin are scorched, and half-charred, like a stick thrust in the fire and withdrawn before the flames seize it. Beside her were two young women, both in the freshness of youth and health. Their faces glowed with a golden-brown, and so great is the effect of colour that their plain features were transfigured. The sunlight under their faces made them beautiful. The summer light had been absorbed by the skin, and now shone from it again; as certain substances exposed to the day absorb light and emit a phosphorescent gleam in the darkness of night, so the sunlight had been drunk up by the surface of the skin, and emanated from it.

Hour after hour in the gardens and orchards they worked in the full beams of the sun, gathering fruit for the London market, resting at midday in the shade of the elms in the corner.

Even then they were in the sunshine – even in the shade, for the air carries it, or its influence, as it carries the perfumes of flowers. The heated air undulates over the field in waves which are visible at a distance; near at hand they are not seen, but roll in endless ripples through the shadows of the trees, bringing with them the actinic power of the sun. Not actinic – alchemic – some intangible, mysterious power which cannot be supplied in any other form but the sun's rays. It reddens the cherry, it gilds the apple, it colours the rose, it ripens the wheat, it touches a woman's face with the golden-brown of ripe life – ripe as a plum. There is no other hue so beautiful as this human sunshine tint.

Richard Jefferies

MEMORIES OF DICKENS

But the *genius loci* of modern Broadstairs is of course Charles Dickens. The aged fishermen on the pier, who can remember him, or say they can, are much to the fore. 'Know'd him? Why, in course I know'd him!' was the prompt reply of a veteran, with his voluminous trousers braced up to his armpits, and his hands up to the elbows in apparently bottomless pockets, whom I accosted quite fortuitously on one occasion. 'Why, my father used to take 'im out in his boat reg'lar, and him lyin' in the bottom all the time a studyin' of 'is book.'

BLEAK HOUSE, BROADSTAIRS

The late 'thirties and most of the 'forties roughly mark the period of Dickens' frequent association with Broadstairs. He seems to have stayed at one time or another in half the houses on the front, according to local tradition. But two of them are directly associated with him. One is an old-fashioned, that is to say, late Georgian-looking lodging house, about the middle of the main front, which bears a tablet recording its well-deserved honour. The other is Bleak House, so called, a now enlarged and turreted villa, standing pleasantly within a garden on the southern point of the Bay, lifted well above the sea. We all know that the Bleak House of the novel was in Hertfordshire. Nor did Dickens even write any part of that work here. But it is quite as interesting to know that he wrote much of *David Copperfield* and other books in the original of the present commodious mansion. Moreover, the original has been preserved by the photographer and shows an astonishingly bare and plain edifice of four storeys, two blank walls and one room thick, suggesting the beginning of a terrace which was never continued. However, it looks solid and comfortable and retired, even then within its own garden.

'This is a little fishing place,' wrote Dickens in 1843 (doubtless from the other house or the *Albion Hotel*, another haunt of his); 'intensely quiet, built on a cliff whereon, in the centre of a tiny semi-circular bay our house stands, the sea rolling and dashing under the windows. Seven miles out are the Goodwin Sands, where floating lights perpetually wink after dark, as if

they were carrying on intrigues with the servants. Under the cliff are rare good sands, where all the children assemble every morning and throw up impossible fortifications, which the sea throws down again at high water. Old gentlemen and ancient ladies flirt after their manner in two reading-rooms and on scattered seats in the open air. In a bay window sits, from nine o'clock until one, a gentleman with rather long hair and no neckcloth, who smiles and grins as if he thought he were very funny indeed. His name is Boz!'

Again in 1837: 'I have walked upon the sands at low water from this place to Ramsgate. I have seen gentlemen and ladies walking upon the earth in slippers of buff and pickling themselves in the sea in complete suits of the same. I have seen short gentlemen looking at nothing through powerful telescopes for hours, and when at last they saw a cloud of smoke, fancying they saw a steamer behind it and going home comfortable and happy.'

There is very little business doing now in Broadstairs harbour, only vessels of very light draft frequent it, though yachts and pleasure boats are, of course, much in evidence. But sea business does not really matter to a place so strong in tourist and residential interests. The sea angler, to be sure, may be descried among the visitors to Broadstairs. He is more profitable perhaps to the boatmen than their own enterprises often prove. But the sea-angling at Broadstairs is not so good as that at Ramsgate, to say nothing of Deal, which is the favourite haunt of the amateur.

OYSTER FISHERMEN, WHITSTABLE

It does not do, however, to tell that to a Broadstairs boatman, as I incidentally discovered in making an incautious remark to that effect to an old-timer as capaciously trousered and as highly braced up as the Dickens gentleman above alluded to.

'Deal!' he almost shouted, 'Deal! Deal's bolstered up; it's just bolstered, and that's all there is about it; it's a noax. Why,' continued he, 'a genleman come 'ere last September, a traveller I thinks he was, and was standin' just where you be now, and he comes up and says,

"Look 'ere," says 'ee, "do you think you could take me where I could catch some fish? I've bin for a week at Deal," says 'ee, "and a-fishin' every day, and ain't catched no more than four fish all the time."

"'Well, guv'nor," says I – for it were a nasty, misty mornin' – "I don't care over much about settin' out in this 'ere weather."

"'Oh," says 'ee, "that amounts to nothin', you just go and git a couple of mackintoshes and a boat and fishin' lines and take me out."

'Well, sir, I took 'im out no further than that there boat yonder, and mind me, sir, we warn't gone no more than a hour and a 'alf, and we brought back two and twenty fine codlin'. And the traveller, when he gits ashore, says to me, says 'ee:

"'D—n Deal!" says 'ee. "Next 'oliday as I gits, it's 'ere I'll come."

"'Guv'nor," says I, "you're right. Deal's bolstered. Deal's a noax." And I says so to you, sir, Deal's a noax.' And having spat vigorously to further emphasize his opinion of Deal, which, not being a sea-fisherman I didn't feel qualified to dispute, we parted.

A. G. Bradley

DISCORDS

One day Kipps set out upon his newly mastered bicycle to New Romney, to break the news of his engagement to his Uncle and Aunt – positively. He was now a finished cyclist, but as yet an unseasoned one; the south-west wind, even in its summer guise, as one meets it in the Marsh, is the equivalent of a reasonable hill, and ever and again he got off and refreshed himself by a spell of walking. He was walking just outside New Romney preparatory to his triumphal entry (one hand off), when abruptly he came upon Ann Pornick.

It chanced he was thinking about her at the time. He had been thinking curious things; whether, after all, the atmosphere of New Romney and the Marsh had not some difference, some faint impalpable quality that was missing in the great and fashionable world of Folkestone behind there on the hill. Here there was a homeliness, a familiarity. He had noted as he passed that old Mr Cliffordown's gate had been mended with a fresh piece of string. In Folkestone he didn't take notice and he didn't care if they built three hundred houses. Come to think of it, that was odd. It was fine and grand to have twelve hundred a year; it was fine to go about on trams and omnibuses and think not a person aboard was as rich as oneself; it was fine to buy and order this and that and never have any work to do, and to be engaged to a girl distantly related to the Earl of Beauprés; but yet there had been a zest in the old time out here, a rare zest in the holidays, in sunlight, on the sea beach, and in the High Street, that failed from these new things. He thought of those bright windows of holiday that had seemed so glorious to him in the retrospect from his apprentice days.

SNARGATE

It was strange that now, amidst his present splendours, they were glorious still!

All those things were over now – perhaps that was it! Something had happened to the world, and the old light had been turned out. He himself was changed, and Sid was changed, terribly changed, and Ann, no doubt, was changed.

He thought of her with the hair blown about her flushed cheeks as they stood together after their race . . .

Certainly she must be changed, and all the magic she had been fraught with to the very hem of her short petticoats gone, no doubt, for ever. And as he thought that, or before and while he thought it – for he came to all these things in his own vague and stumbling way – he looked up, and there was Ann!

She was seven years older, and greatly altered; yet for the moment it seemed to him that she had not changed at all. 'Ann!' he said; and she, with a lifting note,

'It's Art Kipps!'

Then he became aware of changes – improvements. She was as pretty as she had promised to be, her blue eyes as dark as his memory of them, and with a quick, high colour; but now Kipps by several inches was the taller again. She was dressed in a simple gray dress, that showed her very clearly as a straight and healthy little woman, and her hat was Sundayfied, with pink flowers. She looked soft and warm and welcoming. Her face was alight to Kipps with her artless gladness at their encounter.

TRICYCLE, SANDWICH

51

CANTERBURY

'It's Art Kipps!' she said.

'Rather,' said Kipps.

'You got your holidays?'

It flashed upon Kipps that Sid had not told her of his great fortune. Much regretful meditation upon Sid's behaviour had convinced him that he himself was to blame for exasperating boastfulness in that affair, and this time he took care not to err in that direction. So he erred in the other.

'I'm taking a bit of a holiday,' he said.

H.G. Wells

A PLACE OF PILGRIMAGE

The geographical limitations of this little book involve a parting here with any traveller pursuing the Canterbury road to its destination. The historic city itself is not within our compass. It would fill a book, and in truth has filled a good many, besides occupying a considerable share of every History of Kent. The great cathedral alone is a world in itself, both historically and architecturally. The murder of à Becket too still grips the popular imagination, and for the average visitor gives a dramatic finish as it were to his protracted round of the interior. For this is a lengthier and more intricate business than

THE MARKET, CANTERBURY

is involved by a circuit of any other English cathedral, to say nothing of the fact that for obvious historical reasons it should be spiritually the most eloquent. It is good to find what crowds flock daily through it from all parts of the country, and indeed of the earth, during the summer season.

To the better equipped visitor it is of course an insufferable drawback to any right appreciation of a cathedral, this herding system as here, and indeed elsewhere practised, but we must presume it to be unavoidable. Being shoo'd around like a flock of poultry through a succession of locked enclosures, waved about peremptorily within them by even the most amiable verger, and then treated to a set declamation when you have perhaps the best guide-books in your pocket, always strikes me as the most grotesque proceeding. There is not a moment for digesting the facts even if the memory can retain them, or still less for that undisturbed recognition of the significance with which they endow the historic spot of ground you may be treading. I speak impersonally, but I am sure that most of us feel a little touch of needless humiliation as we obey the various words of command and meekly listen to the verger's set oration. For myself, I always feel sorry for the orator himself, which of course I know to be absurd. I have known a good many vergers and have a high respect for their calling. Which sentiment, however, in no way prevents one's sense of the ridiculous from being deeply stirred on an inappropriate occasion by this part of the duties laid upon them by Deans and Chapters.

But all this merely leads up to the fact that when any thus conducted group arrives at the scene of the famous Archbishop's murder, which is vividly described in detail by the guide, there is a marked quickening of interest. The laggards step up to the front, the bored or those peradventure sacrific-

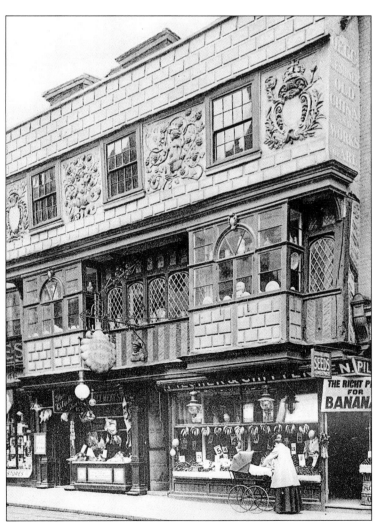

HIGH STREET, CANTERBURY

LAMBERHURST

ing themselves on the altar of friendship cock their ears and feel no doubt that they are now getting something for their sixpences. To the rank and file it is no doubt the grand climax of the tour. If the saint no longer fills the inns of Canterbury, he is still a great personality to the modern pilgrim perambulating the cathedral.

A. G. Bradley

OLD WAYS AND OLD DAYS

The simpler life of the old days was not without certain charm. Domestic duties were thought worthy; a good manager was praised. Most modern canons of health were violated, yet a healthy, hardy race seemed none the worse for this neglect.

In spite of negligences and ignorances men and women were sent into the world of life with character and grit; succeeding generations will not do badly if they come near them in both.

Advertisement as we know it today did not exist. The good wine needed no bush. Log-rolling had not been invented, and if Nepotism could be discerned, why blame it? Today there is plenty of wild and flowery talk about heredity; it is possible

that the relations of a worthy man (or a man who has got on) may be the best people to fill favoured billets. Anyway they are likely to prove as able and useful as men selected by competitive examination.

Teaching was an unknown art. Learning, scholarship, and the command of mental and moral powers were appreciated and cultivated.

The head of the house was master; his wife, mistress. Fathers and mothers were not intimate or familiar with their children, and exacted obedience and deference. The children were none the worse for this.

Servants were not birds of passage. In many old country houses, the head nurse began life as a nursery-maid and the cook as a helper in the kitchen (a rank below scullery-maid). These servants would remain in the same family, marry generally some one on the estate, bring up their children, and then return to end their days in service as upper servants. In many old country houses this was the history of the butler and housekeeper or head nurse. These old servants knew the family in a way hard to understand nowadays. Its interest was their interest, its welfare their welfare. When the young master buckled on his sword and went to the wars, his soldier man was in many cases his foster-brother, the son of a woman who felt almost a blood relationship. And when the bride left her home, the girl who accompanied her was, as a rule, the

SERVANTS

daughter of her mother's woman. The word 'maid' was not used for the capable elderly woman who waited upon the mistress. Bess McGaw was always spoken of as Mrs Orme's woman. Or the girl might be the daughter of the old and valued humble friends, the head nurse or the housekeeper.

The human family was linked together closer in these past times, no slight matter. The spirit of 'Jack as good or better than his master' was then dormant. It was not class against class, but class with class working for mutual good. There is no going back, the present must be lived, the future faced. But with honest and good intent and unswerving principle, the present may be lived worthily, and the future can be met with a dauntless spirit.

Jane Connolly

HOW THE IRON-ROAD CAME TO KENT

The stock grumble of the Man of Kent or Kentish Man, is his railway service. It has always been the reserve joke for every comic paper when short of copy. The railway service may, or may not be, all that is desired, but there are worse.

Still that is nothing to do with our subject, for this I can say, that the history of the coming of the Iron-road into Kent, is as interesting a story as can be found in the annals of the County.

It is one of bitter opposition on the part of the very people who were ultimately to receive the greatest benefits, the landowners!; senseless ridicule from those whom we should have credited with more wisdom, and above all a triumphant fight of engineering skill against great natural difficulties.

RAILWAYMEN

The construction of a railway through the county was first projected in 1825, surveys were then made and also again in 1832 and 1835.

The promoters of a railway from London to Dover examined the country on the north side of the county, but the idea met with no local encouragement from the towns and only violent opposition from the landed proprietors. Today all the public authorities are constantly beseeching for better facilities of transit.

The difficulties of the engineer were many and varied; it was feared at one time it would be impossible for any engines to surmount the gradients of the Kentish Hills. The passage of the Medway at Rochester was considered a barrier almost insurmountable, and those who had the guardianship of the bridge, shrank from even communicating with individuals who could be so wildly speculative as to propose a railway from London to Dover.

The force of circumstances was too great and in 1833 the idea of a railway through north Kent was abandoned.

Attention was next turned to the making of a line through mid Kent via Maidstone, but the same senseless opposition arose. Maidstone declared unanimously against, not only the line in question but against any railway whatever through Kent. This set-back appeared at first to be fatal to the Kentish railway, but another opening offered viz.: by making use of the London and Croydon Railway and so entering the county through Surrey.

This was eventually done and the South Eastern Railway commenced their line at the termination of the Croydon Railway.

A marked difference was shewn by the inhabitants of the district through which it was now proposed the new line should traverse via Tunbridge and the Weald of Kent; every support was accorded and the work at last went ahead.

It makes us smile nowadays to read of the opposition tactics, but when we realize what the county had lost through the hindrances placed in the way of progress, we are more inclined to weep. Maidstone must, as a town, often feel inclined to kick itself, for had the original idea been carried out, it would now have been an important main-line station, with many of the fast trains to Dover stopping there, instead of its irritating stop-at-all-stations service of trains.

Will Syms

HOP PICKERS, YALDING

DESPERATE ENCOUNTER WITH A BULL

Desperate Encounter with a Bull. – a shocking occurrence has taken place at the residence of Sir E. Scott, Sunbridge Park Farm. It appears that, on Monday evening, when the cowman, Lush, was seeing to the cattle for the night, a very valuable bull, known to be of a spirited character, broke his chain, and getting loose, rushed into the yard, and attacked him. The unfortunate man did his best, for some time, to keep the bull off, but it followed him, goring him and tossing him up round the yard time after time. As he was unable to make his escape, he screamed for help, and a carpenter, named Kendall, working on the estate, ran to his assistance. The bull now left Lush for a time, and turning on Kendall, tossed and gored him to such an extent, that, in a very short time, his arm was broken, and he was rendered perfectly helpless. The district postman, named Turner, now came through the yard, and the bull turned upon him. He, however, managed to make his escape, and went for assistance. In the meantime, the bull kept following Kendall, and, had not timely help arrived, he, too, would soon have been killed. He was, at length, rescued, and, while they were carrying him out of the yard, the furious animal again turned on the unfortunate man Lush, and killed him.

The Maidstone and Kent County Standard

THE GREEN GARDEN

A poem of 1776 (too bad to be worth quoting) shows that the immigrant pickers were then vilely housed. They were vilely housed in 1897, when, through lack of any attempt at sanitation, the streams were polluted and Maidstone decimated by typhoid. The average 'hopper-hut' was a sort of small, damp, wooden bathing-machine, usually placed on the lower slope of a garden, so that the soil drained well into them. There were some of brick, and these often had the advantage of a communal fire and cooking-room; but even they were no better than stables, and usually not so large nor so clean.

Into those astonishing hotels the guests flocked. Of old the journey was usually made by road. Polhill and River Hill, Wrotham Hill, in the early autumn were black and resonant with all manner of uncouth vehicles, drawn by four-legged beasts which it would often be difficult to call horses, finding their way, with a gipsy certainty, to Wateringbury, Farleigh, the Suttons, Staplehurst, Tenterden, and East Kent itself. High piled, domestic gear would tower among a welter of babies and children. They still travel that route; but more now go by the special trains to Paddock Wood, the Charing Cross of their distribution through West and Mid Kent and the Weald; or to Canterbury for the East.

In the time of my youth there was, perhaps, something to be said for the attitude of mind which treated them as brute and

57

DOCKYARD, CHATHAM

alien beasts. Even today, when conditions are infinitely better, they are not country folk, though they may have recurred to the same farm and the same garden for a generation, and perhaps their fathers before them. Thirty years ago (when in Kent we still rejoiced in election riots, and Bluey got his head broken by an imported Radical) the variously coloured Lions and Dragons, the Kings, Queens, and fabulous monsters, would be strewn as to their approaches with tired children, and filled as to their interior maws with parents of both sexes getting drunk as they had earned the power to be. The police, reinforced for the occasion – there were as many as three in a thousand-population village - had often a rough time. I have seen viragoes, half-stripped, fighting in the street with broken bottles. I walked a long six miles once with a dirty little rogue whose head had been cut open by an incensed rival a day or two before. He was going to report himself to the police, for he was on ticket-of-leave. His bandage was not very clean, but I wish he had not taken it off to show me the injuries.

Yet he was vivid and human; and the amount of goodness and courage in a garden picked by Londoners is not short of enormous. You come back here again to a simple socialism, even if, for reasons of policy, the local people and the foreigners are always allotted to different gardens. Today the immigrants are helped intimately by their neighbours of all ranks; the babies are tended, and gentlefolk aid the picking to swell the Londoners' (and their own people's) earnings. Many families now come for a whole succession of crops, from the cherry through the hop to the apple. You may find them at another season selling flowers in Piccadilly Circus, or rubbish on a barrow in Aldgate. They will remember you.

E. Harvey Darton

A SOLDIER'S CHILD

In Chatham, a soldier's child could not fail to become acutely army conscious. Of the navy too, for that matter, since it was a dockyard as well as a garrison town, and one of my most thrilling early experiences was of being taken all over the as yet uncommissioned *Rodney* – one of the new *Admiral* class, all fresh paint and knobby steel plating – and asking where with all this offensive paraphernalia she was going out to fight, and being told by my nurse,

'Oh, somewhere in the East, I suppose.'

Even more thrilling was it to see a steam hammer pounding a great sparking mass of white-hot metal: coming down on it, one somehow felt, with the whole weight of Queen Victoria's authority, that no foreigner – which to me would have been equivalent to Frenchman – would ever be mad enough to challenge. The Kings of old, who had led their peoples to those battles far and wide that my nurse used to sing about, had never anything like this at their disposal. She might be too kind an old lady to go in for this sort of thing without due provocation – but by Jingo if she did! Which was a thought to make an English child sleep quiet in his cot.

But naturally, for me, it was the army that occupied the foreground of the picture,

> The army that fights for the Queen,
> The very best army that ever was seen!

and certainly it was an incomparably more picturesque and colourful army than anything you can imagine today. It was, moreover, conspicuously under royal patronage: for no circus, nor even the Salvation Army, then in its youthful prime, that

CHATHAM

put down a glorious drumfire barrage once a week under my nursery window, could vie for entertainment with what seem to me to have been the fairly frequent occasions on which His Royal Highness, the Duke of Cambridge, came down in his capacity of Commander-in-Chief, to review the Chatham Brigade. As our house was right above the station, we could see his whole cavalcade mounting and getting under way – the expression 'glittering staff' was certainly no misnomer, with the whole street in spate with cocked hats and scarlet and decorations; and when the grand old warrior led it under the railway bridge, it almost seemed as if his whiskers would have brushed the brick work on either side.

It was always possible – for there was nothing hurried about the Duke's proceedings – to get to a convenient vantage point in plenty of time to see the very best army that ever was seen showing what it could, and would, do against a real enemy.

As one who had been habituated to play soldiers, to think soldiers, and to daydream himself a soldier, I kept an almost photographic impression of that spectacle, and it explained much since to me that would otherwise have been obscure. The battle-field was a magnificent open space called the Lines, with the ground from the South edge falling abruptly down to the valley in which lie Rochester and the Medway. It was somewhere on the Lines that my uncle Renny Tailyour had made his record hit for 13 without an overthrow; for in those strenuous days there were no boundaries, and only *bona fide* lost balls. When last I visited Chatham the glory had departed from the Lines, for it all seemed to have been enclosed and cut up into ignoble snippets.

It was along that edge that the enemy had taken up his position, having presumably climbed up out of the valley, and lain down for a breather. I say 'his' – but as a matter of fact there

were at least ten of him, each man being supposed to represent a hundred. I did not suppose any such thing. It was only fitting that the Queen's forces should exceed these Frenchmen, as I visualized them, in quantity no less than in quality.

It was on this devoted ten, lying conspicuously on their stomachs – for there seemed to be no question of entrenching – that the whole Chatham garrison staged a long, leisurely attack over ground suggestive of a billiard table. Undeterred by the massacre of the Prussian Guard at St Privat under rather similar circumstances 18 years previously, they advanced in three closely packed and accurately dressed scarlet lines, lying down at frequent intervals, as much, I imagine, for the purpose of correcting their alignment as of popping off blanks. In the second or third line a score or so of men would ever and anon spring simultaneously to their feet to discharge an equally simultaneous volley. I should think that under these circumstances even ten men, counting one as one, with a sufficient number of cartridges, could have accounted with their Martinis for a greater part of the assailants; unless they had been conspicuously bad shots, which, under His Royal Highness's system of training, they most likely were, since a straight shot was accounted as nothing in his eye compared with a straight line.

However, at long last, the spoil-sport bugles went, just as the final charge was being prepared and the invaders were about to be bayoneted and pitchforked, before my delighted eyes, over the crest. Then the victors formed up intact, and with the bands thundering out the regimental tunes, marched triumphantly past the Duke, who I think must have enjoyed this part of it most of all. For peace-time soldiering it was the most impressive spectacle that anyone could conceive. But when something of the same sort had been tried against a rab-

THE CARRIER'S VAN

ble of unsoldierly Boers, not so long before, there had been a rather different tale to tell! But that would be no bar to its being tried again, in due course, against the selfsame enemy.

Of course it will be said that a small child was perfectly incapable of appreciating the deep motives behind all this martial pageantry. And that would have been true; for I had no idea at the time of the mastering anxiety that possessed the staff and the commanders, which was that on no account whatever should proceedings be prolonged for a single second beyond the hour fixed for HRH's lunch, which always consisted of chop and tomato sauce. Any failure in this respect would be notified to all concerned in royally unpublishable terms, for the Duke had inherited from his uncles, of the Regency generation, a command of varied and picturesque imagery far beyond the resources of Billingsgate.

Esmé Wingfield Stratford

JOHN HOMEWARD – THE CARRIER

I seldom spoke to anyone while I was out for my walks, but now and again I would meet John Homeward, the carrier, on his way back from the county town where he went three days a week. Homeward was a friendly man: I always 'passed the time of day' with him. He was a keen cricketer and one of Dixon's chief cronies. The weather and the next year's cricket were the staple topics of our conversation. Homeward had been making his foot-pace journeys with his hooded van and nodding horse ever since I could remember, and he seemed an essential feature of the ten miles across the Weald to Ashridge (a somnolent town which I associated with the smell of a brewery and the grim fact of people being hung in the gaol there). All the year round, whether there was snow on the ground or blossom on the fruit trees, the carrier's van crawled across the valley with its cargo of utilities, but Homeward was

WATTLE LOAD, SANDWICH

always alone with his horse, for he never took passengers. In my mind's eye he is invariably walking beside his van, for he always got out at the steep hill which winds down to the Weald. His burly figure and kindly bearded face must have gone up and down that hill about five thousand times before he retired to prosper with a small public-house. I used to wonder what he thought about while on the road, for he had the look of a man who was cogitant rather than vegetative. Dixon told me that he spent his whole time weighing the pros and cons of the half-crown bets which he made on races. In matters connected with the Turf he was a compendium of exact knowledge, and his profession allowed him ample leisure to make up his mind about likely outsiders and nicely handicapped horses at short odds.

Siegfried Sassoon

BIRLING

61

AYLESFORD BRIDGE

THE PARISH CLERK

In former days when the general custom was to change into the Geneva gown to preach, and the sermon was often an hour long, the parson and the clerk often used to take refreshment before the sermon in the vestry, and one of the long Tate and Brady Psalms at the end of the Prayer Book used to be chosen to give time for the meal. On one of these occasions it is said the clerk's wife, who was a good cook, brought into the vestry by the outer door some dumplings, which the parson and clerk enjoyed to their satisfaction, when the clerk reminded the parson that they were singing the last verse of the psalm. I must remind you here that this was in the days of the old three deckers, and the Geneva gown had wide sleeves, and the parson as a rule gesticulated much with his face and arms. Hearing the unpleasant news from his clerk, the parson snatched up two of the remaining dumplings and put them in his sleeve, and the clerk put the other two in his coat tail pocket. Getting hot in his sermon the parson gesticulated as usual, and in doing so shook one of the dumplings from his sleeve, which fell on the clerk's bald head; again he gesticulated, and again another dumpling fell on the functionary below. This last time he rose from his seat and, taking the dumplings out of his coat pocket, threw them at the parson, exclaiming: 'Oh, that's your little game – it's my turn now.' We do not know where or when this actually happened, but amongst other places Maidstone has been credited with it . . .

Two more more tales of Clerks of more recent times we will tell. One of the old Clerk of Bicknor-cum-Huckinge, when Mr Twopenny took the living some fifty years ago. In his predecessor's time the Church of Huckinge had never been used. Mr Twopenny, having called a meeting of his parishioners, said he was going to take service in each church alternatively. 'Next Sunday', he added, 'in the morning I shall take duty at Bicknor Church, and in the afternoon at Huckinge; the next Sunday in the morning at Huckinge and in the afternoon at Bicknor.'

'Then you won't,' said the old parish clerk from the audience .

'But I shall,' replied the Vicar.

'Then,' said the Clerk, 'you can't preach.'

The Vicar, much astonished, answered, 'I can preach.'

The Clerk again replied, 'Not from 'Uckinge pulpit'.

The clergyman once more answered, 'I shall preach in Huckinge Church from the pulpit next Sunday afternoon.'

'Ah, but I noo ye can't,' said the Clerk, 'for my old 'en turkey's a sitting up there!'

Some years ago, when I was Curate of West Peckham, the old clerk there was a seaman who had served in the Black Fleet in the Russian war. Noticing him one Sunday chewing in church, and having been told that many of his calling, when they did this, spat all over the church, besides thinking that chewing in church was irreverent, I determined to stop him. A golden opportunity arrived. My brother bought me some real made up Royal Navy tobacco. I offered this to the old man on condition that he should not chew in church. He said, 'Why not?' And I first told him how dirty it was to spit about the church. He dumbfounded me with the answer, 'Lor', Sir, I never spits; I keep it till it's consoomed.'

Well a truce to the ashes of the old Parish Clerk. We still have visions of him in a long tail coat and little white choker, instructing the young curate or the new vicar or rector in the

LYCH GATE, BUCKLAND CHURCH, DOVER

vestry in matters wherein he held himself a Solomon, and they but poor uninformed or partly informed dolts. Still so insisting in his having a part was he in every way as to have been married both as man and maid to numbers of the opposite sex by saying 'I will', and to be godfather of all the children in the parish from the Squire's heir and heiress and the parson's children, to the babies of the cottager and the wayfarer. The Parish Clerk as a reality is a thing of the past; he is gone; vergers and other named officials have taken his place, but never fill it as he did. Let us end by saying: '*Requiescat in pace. Amen.*'

Philo Cantii

CHILDHOOD AND YOUTH

The subject of this memoir dates his individuality back into the reigns of four English Sovereigns having been born on February 28th 1829. His father survived this somewhat interesting event only six short years – what might, or might not, have been the Son but for the untoward slipping of an axe in the woods adjoining Cobham Park, who shall say! It left him however, fatherless at a very tender age, and to be sole charge of a most truly pious, and devoted Mother. 'John and Edward' – these were the last words of the dying father to his elder brother, and himself on the last morning of his existence which he has always recollected – 'Be sure that you always obey your Mother.'

My Mother however was assisted in the general guardianship of her children, and especially in the management of the Cobham Hall Estate by my Uncle John Bligh and my uncle

THE HON. REVD EDWARD VESEY BLIGH AND FAMILY

COBHAM HALL

(by marriage) Dr Longley, then Headmaster of Harrow (later on successively Bishop of Ripon, Durham, and Archbishop of York and Canterbury). It may be as well perhaps to mention here in this connection that the guardianship was not a mere formal matter – and led to an amicable lawsuit (Bligh v Bligh) in connection with my Mother's connection with the followers of Irving at Chatham, and elsewhere, when the Court of Chancery issued an order that myself and the other children must be brought up in the religion of the father, i.e. according to the principles and doctrines of the Church of England. This is also a suitable opportunity for testifying that my good Mother was the most conscientious person – even to a fault if I may say so – that I ever came across – she was thoroughly sound and correct upon all the beliefs, and important doctrines of the Church of England, and her Irvingite views were a kind of super structure which did not at all inconvenience her in attending the Church Services, when she had not the opportunity of going elsewhere, but she gave her literal *tenth* part of income to the Irvingite Body all her life long, I feel sure, which would be from £250 to £300 per annum. She died in March 1884, just short of her 80th year leaving the most fragrant of memories behind her.

The Hon. Revd Edward Vesey Bligh

RELIGIOUS IMPRESSIONS

I introduce this subject next: of course in itself, it comes first and foremost but as the domestic considerations to which I have already alluded had an important bearing on my exchanging the Diplomatic for the Clerical profession, this may be the most convenient place to introduce the subject.

I go back at once to my tenderest years under the immediate surveillance and methodical discipline of my tender loving Mother – She was however the personification of a severe conscientiousness which stopped little short of applying to her babes the letter of the law of Sinai: I can recollect she dwelt upon passages in the Book of Proverbs 'he that spareth the rod hateth his child' and others such like and how with most apparent unmercifulness she or the 'chief butler' acting for her applied the birch with stripes almost unceasing – and all for conscience sake. I am sure she would have walked through plateglass or through the fire simply for the same reason. Suffice it to say that neither I nor any of my brothers and sisters perished under treatment which possibly I may have somewhat exaggerated now. In those days no doubt the role of parents and tutors was by fear chiefly after the fashion of the Headmaster of Eton Dr Keate who is said to have on one occasion flogged all the boys himself; the rule of love on the

MARKET SQUARE, DOVER

other hand was but little understood. In my Mother's case however the love behind the floggings made all the difference, for if, in the ordinary relationships of life there ever was a pious, gentle, good, perfectly straightforward and just, unselfish and self-denying and withal loving more than any other woman it was my own Sainted Mother, Emma Jane, Countess of Darnley – I was brought up thus to later years somewhat ultra legally as I have said too much under Sinai, too little under Zion.

I recollect that particular Summer very well because during a Match (Kent v Surrey) at Kensington Oval I was taken suddenly in the field very ill of ague; and for some weeks 'on and off, it' at my Mother's house alternate days, and being gradually reduced to vanishing point by an old fashioned Rhubarb and Magnesia doctor: and my recovery was both sudden and grotesque under the auspices of my old friend General Gascoigne, who to my Mother's horror called for me one Sunday morning to accompany him to Tunbridge Wells – the somewhat doubtful state of this proceeding being – a cure from change of air – It answered however under God's blessing admirably – It was my good day. When I started and upon the next (the bad day) I had no return, and I soon afterwards recovered – My dear Mother, I am afraid never quite forgot although no doubt she forgave, the good natured interference with my private affairs, and I don't think the former most intimate friendship with the Gascoignes was ever quite the same afterwards.

It was in this year and not so very long after this ague that I can record the very best performance at cricket of which I was ever guilty at Canterbury in the match between the Gentlemen of Kent, and the Gentlemen of England – when no doubt I won the match by my own individual batting; that too in the palmy days of England's 'quickest bowler as ever was' Harvey Fellows – Just as a matter of proportion – I will not say comparison as there is no real means of comparing cricket now and cricket then and I will say that my own second innings (not out) 44 as applied to anyone else of the same period would be fully and more than fully equal to 144 in the present day – The grounds have made all the difference between a billiard table, and a mowed lawn and legs are used shamelessly to defend a wicket where Bats were only thought of then. – Must now close this chapter which I have denominated 'Childhood & Youth'. Being 21 years of age, and launched upon the public service of the Queen abroad I may claim to have become a Man.

From Dover to Birling; from Birling to Cobham and so on – with my Mother sometimes – we spent the first months of 1855 and I was ordained in London by old Murray, the last of the old-fashioned wigged Bishops, in March of that year. He was a good old sort, though not much of a theologian. I remember well my preliminary visit to him at Danbury Palace near Chelmsford where I stayed at least the night, if not more, and played chess with him after dinner. The conversation

turned on Wouldham, to which he had first appointed a nephew as Rector. Old Bishop Murray was no smoker and had a keen horror of tobacco! 'Yes' said he to me 'it is true I have appointed Mr – to Wouldham. But oh! if I had only known – what do you think – why that when he came here the other day to be instituted he actually smoked in his Bedroom! – he would never have had that Living!' Of course I was much amused. I however put in a good word for the Nephew saying I had always heard that Wouldham was a frightful place for ague and it was probably a necessity that a man should smoke there.

On the 24th November, however, things came to a crisis in the domestic line, and a son and heir to the fortunes of Bligh-Nevill – whatever these might be – was born – the very ugliest and sparest babby which, in the words of his maternal Grandmother, she ever did see! It was a mere bag of bones with a physiognomy indicative of the Darwin Ape theory – and I suppose in this case must have come into the world of mankind somewhat unfurnished and prematurely. At any rate the said Grandmother who was to have officiated as Chief Lady of the Bedchamber, was not yet installed in office and was considerably surprised at its early venture. It is fair towards the Infant here to state that it soon outgrew the starvation process or appearance and has developed since with the more than ordinary bone and muscle – leave looks alone – has married and become Paterfamilias, M.F.H. M.H., J.P., County XI Cricketer and has I believe served on Grand and Special Jury!

. . . To show how easy going Bishops were then I say I was ordained on no bona fide Title at all – The dear old Vicar of Cobham (father of Edward and Sir John, Mr Stokes, commonly called in our family 'The Doctor' gave me one pro forma (I obtained a real one at Snodland almost immediately afterwards of which more presently). It so happened that the head gardener (Wilkinson) a little portly man who used to dress habitually in a blue tailcoat with brass buttons died just then, and I think his funeral was about the first ecclesiastical rite that I ever performed; and though it was a little later on – perhaps a year or two – I may as well mention it here – it fell to my lot to bury the dear old 'Doctor' himself who had so kindly befriended me with a Title – Hence it came to pass that we Father, Mother and Baby, took up our quarters in a very tiny habitation near the Bull Inn and the old turnpike at Snodland –

A more undesirable locale for my own ideas could not well be; far worse now with 4,000 people, but it was then in its Babyhood too, and I think the population nearly all cement and limeburners, was little over 700. Quite flat – smoky without a single real gentleman much less lady in tow, lot of people in the social scale, the one redeeming point was the close neighbourhood of Birling Manor, where at any rate was a refuge for the aristocratic curate's wife – The old Rector of Snodland was a positive curiosity – quite an old fossil, an antique Bachelor who lived in two small rooms of his rectory tended by a beaming housekeeper called 'Kitty.' Mr Phelps – that was his name, was nearly eighty years of age – a very short man – dressed always in a long tail coat nearly down to his ankles – with an old fashioned white choker round and round his neck several times – a very big tall hat well to the back of his head – and a 'Mother Gamp' large umbrella. On Sundays, he wore his University gown, which he had at Oxford or Cambridge 50 years ago and which from black to brown had lapsed into a dingy floor colour; he always marched down the village on his way to Church and back again in this manner.

I must here relate one very old story which he himself told me. – He was a great foe to *Smugglers*, of whom in the old times there were many, and he had taken a somewhat leading part against them. – Now Mr Phelps was in the habit of walk-

HIGH STREET, ROCHESTER

ing one day in the week across the Medway via Wouldham to Rochester, and back again – a walk of many miles – Very likely he may have been known to go to his bankers on such a day, but anyhow he was a marked man as the sequel will show. – Fortunately for Mr Phelps – unfortunately for another individual, a certain Tailor in Rochester – also a diminutive man of small physique, the latter took it into his head to walk towards Snodland, through some woods where the path lay, and coming along unwittingly was pounced upon by one or more of the smugglers party, and cruelly murdered then and there – by mistake of course, but a very convenient one for Mr Phelps who had that day left Rochester somewhat later on his return walk to Snodland. Suspicion seems to have fallen upon the right party, and at the Coroner's inquest on the tailor which was held at Custon, Mr Phelps was chosen foreman – his would-be murderer being also present under arrest, and the two facing each other. I recollect how the old gentleman narrated to me his own feelings at the time under such extraordinary circumstances knowing well he was himself the 'corpus' intended, over which the Inquest was being held – It was satis-

factory however that the murderer was so promptly brought to justice, and in due course so duly hanged.

One more little anecdote of my old Rector – On Quarter days when my Stipend of £25 was due, the old gentleman would triumphantly march up the Village to my house, and put the money down in hard cash or otherwise, and good naturedly dispose of his debt for my humble services, as if I was the biggest 'dun' or 'Old Clothes' London Jew craving for a prompt settlement! He also solemnly confused me when I first took up duty – no reflection of course on the sermon which I preached subsequently – as to the proper length for such discussion using the phrase as I well remember as also my astonishment 'Twelve minutes is long enough for any Monkey to be talking to a lot of others.' Peculiar indeed and hardly encouraging exhortation to a newly ordained Deacon coming to work in a parish for the first time! Old Phelps however was a character and the oldest clergyman in the diocese.

The Hon. Revd Edward Vesey Bligh

THE BOYS' PLAYGROUND

RUCKINGE CHURCH

GREAT EXPECTATIONS

My father's family name being Pirrip, and my Christian name Phillip, my infant tongue could make of both names nothing longer or more explicit than Pip. So, I called myself Pip, and came to be called Pip.

I give Pirrip as my father's family name, on the authority of his tombstone and my sister – Mrs Joe Gargery, who married the blacksmith. As I never saw my father or my mother, and never saw any likeness of either of them (for their days were long before the days of photographs), my first fancies regarding what they were like, were unreasonably derived from their tombstones. The shape of the letters on my father's, gave me an odd idea that he was a square, stout, dark man, with curly black hair. From the character and turn of the inscription, 'Also Georgiana Wife of the Above,' I drew a childish conclusion that my mother was freckled and sickly. To five little stone lozenges, each about a foot and a half long, which were arranged in a neat row beside their grave, and were sacred to the memory of five little brothers of mine – who gave up trying to get a living exceedingly early in that universal struggle – I am indebted for a belief I religiously entertained that they had all been born on their backs with their hands in their trouser-pockets, and had never taken them out in this state of existence.

Ours was the marsh country, down by the river, within, as the river wound, twenty miles of the sea. My first most vivid and broad impression of the identity of things, seems to me to have been gained on a memorable raw afternoon towards evening. At such a time I found out for certain, that this bleak place overgrown with nettles was the churchyard; and that Philip Pirrip, late of this parish, and also Georgiana wife of the above, were dead and buried; and that Alexander, Bartholomew, Abraham, Tobias, and Roger, infant children of the aforesaid, were also dead and buried; and that the dark flat wilderness beyond the church-yard, intersected with dykes and mounds and gates, with scattered cattle feeding on it, was the marshes; and that the low leaden line beyond was the river; and that the distant savage lair from which the wind was rushing, was the sea; and that the small bundle of shivers growing afraid of it all and beginning to cry, was Pip.

Charles Dickens

69

APPLEDORE

APPLEDORE

The marshy district known as Dowles was at one time responsible for giving Appledore a reputation for unhealthiness. The large tract of country, seven hundred acres in extent, was in wet seasons either a dismal swamp or totally submerged, and in consequence caused much sickness. The malady was of the character of malarial fever and so malignant that the inhabitants of the surrounding neighbourhood were recognized by their pitted faces. This same land is now drained by the Commissioners of Romney Marsh by means of a powerful pump, which can throw as much as forty tons of water a minute. The pumping station stands adjoining the Canal, into which the water is turned and conveyed to the sea at Dymchurch. In addition to draining the Dowles the pump is capable of relieving the flat country around Snargate of much of the water which comes from the hills in wet weather. Thanks to this excellent system of drainage Marsh ague, which can still be remembered with dread by many of the inhabitants, and which filled nearly every house with sickness at certain periods of the year, is now unknown. Why, Appledore is now one of the healthiest spots in Kent. Walking down the village street this spring I met an old man going gaily along, the very picture of health. Yet I was assured that in his youth he was a miserable, ague-stricken being; now he looked as happy as a sandboy, had reached his eightieth birthday, and looked like seeing another twenty. And next I met a skittish damsel of eighty-four! She, too, remembered the pallid cheeks of seventy years ago, 'but,' she added, 'things is changed since de Dowles was drainded.' So much for Science in her fight against Nature.

Charles Igglesden

DEATH OMENS

During my rambles up and down the county, I have met with several peculiar superstitions in regard to approaching death, some of which are new to me, although, possibly they may be well known to others. Passing over the 'dog howling' and death watch omens, which are widely distributed, I will give one or two examples of less common beliefs.

Very frequently white spots may be observed on photographs, the result, probably, of some neglect on the part of the photographer. The superstitious, however, regard these 'spotty' marks from another point of view. They say they are portentive of the death of the person whose likeness they represent. I have met with this particular belief in places so far apart as Broadstairs, Gravesend, and Woolwich, but, taking into consideration the date of the invention of photography, it must indeed be quite a latter-day superstition.

A 'limp' corpse is held to be a sure sign of another death in the family. I know a man who is daily expecting to hear bad news of this nature from the fact that his brother, whom he lost recently, was extraordinarily 'limp' after death.

Some time ago, a Northfleet woman was plucking a pair of pigeons in her house, when a neighbour called in, who at once pointed out how unlucky it was to have pigeons' feathers in the house, declaring that it was a sure sign of death to follow in that house. This superstition is akin to another common belief in various parts of our land, viz., if a sick person eagerly desire a dish of pigeons to eat, it presages his near decease.

I should like to be informed whether the omens mentioned above prevail in other counties.

Rambler

RECULVER, NEAR HERNE BAY

THE RECULVER

Little more than half a century ago, before the old ruins were more fully protected by the Brethren of the Trinity House, many ghastly relics were washed out of the crumbling church yard. Quite recently acorns – one with its cap still adhering – ebon [dark] with age were brought up from the bottom some distance from the shore, but the graves are no longer rifled by the sea, as they were when Douglas Jerrold, sojourner at the ancient village of Herne, wrote his essay, 'A Gossip at Reculvers':

> One day, wandering near this open graveyard, we met a boy, carrying away, with exulting looks, a skull in very perfect preservation. He was a London boy, and looked rich indeed with his treasure.
>
> 'What have you there?' we asked.
> 'A man's head – a skull,' was the answer.
> 'And what can you possibly do with a skull?'
> 'Take it to London.'
> 'And when you have it in London, what then will you do with it?'
> 'I know.'
> 'No doubt. But what will you do with it?'
> And to this thrice repeated question, the boy three times answered 'I know.'
> 'Come, here's sixpence. Now, what will you do with it?' The boy took the coin – grinned – hugged himself, hugging the skull the closer, and said very briskly – 'Make a money-box of it.'

A strange thought for a child. And yet, mused we as we strolled along, how many of us, with nature beneficent and smiling on all sides, how many of us think of nothing so much as hoarding sixpences – yes, hoarding them even in the very jaws of desolate Death.

Walter Jerrold

DIALECT

But some doubt seems to have been expressed by those whom Dr Ellis consulted as to whether the contrary use of v for w obtained in Kent. It is, however, quite certain that this usage, though rapidly becoming obsolete, is still to be met with here and there. An old man living near Westenhanger said to the present writer with a hearty laugh, 'I have a cousin comes here sometimes and amuses us all. He calls this place Vestenhanger. He lives in the "veskit" district you know,' he added by way of explanation. It turned out that this cousin came from near Wingham. (The worthy old fellow who was so much amused with his relative's Vestenhanger saw nothing funny in his own *wery*, *weal* (veal), and *winegar*.) It is worth noting, too, that even in his own district people speak of Postling Vents, instead of *Wents*, or roads. And the writer has heard a Folkestone fisherman call a friend Vellard (Wellard). But this cockneyism – as it may be called – everyone will recall Dickens' 'Samivel Veller' – is rapidly dropping out of use in most parts of the county. Before leaving the pronunciation – and we have indicated but a very few of its peculiarities – two general charac-

NORTH STREET, ASHFORD

teristics may be pointed out. First the *vowel* sounds are almost without exception remarkably *impure*, or rather, *undecided*. The *i* in *milk*, for instance, is a sort of cross between the short *e* and the short *u*, *mel'k* or *mul'k*. *Past* is neither clearly *pahst* nor *păst*, but a peculiar half-way, so to speak, between the two, *paest*, which must be heard to be appreciated. The *a* for *o*, *oi* for *i*, *u* for *oo*, and so forth have already been noted. The second great characteristic of the Kentish provincial pronunciation is a very remarkable clipping out or jumbling together of syllables, which renders the dialect at first very puzzling to a stranger.

It rarely happens that three or four consecutive words are uttered *complete*; some one or more portions are sure to be left out: 'Ae paes tiw' does duty for 'half-past two', '*goozbriz*' for gooseberries, 'Satdy' (or Setdy) for Saturday, 'Eshf' (or 'Eshfd') for Ashford, 'bar' for barrow. At the railway stations, 'mornpeyp' stands for morning papers, 'scursh', with a faint soupçon of an *n* at the end, passes for excursion. Such a rapid jumble as 'moilgooberrneez' (!) for 'mine will go better than his,' may be constantly heard from the street boys. The effect of all this is very striking, and teachers know the difficulty there is sometimes in getting children to read without slurring over or dropping two-thirds of the syllables. Thus the sentence 'A collision between ourselves and the natives now seemed inevitable', will sometimes be read something like this, 'clizh-twee-seln-nate-now-see-nevl,' with a faint 'filling in', so to speak, between these strongly marked syllables.

Of the grammar little need be said here, but a few curious turns of expression may be noted. Double negatives are extremely common, and such phrases as 'no more you don't,' 'no more I didn't,' are everywhere heard. Then we get 'you didn't ought to,' for 'you ought not,' 'he don't dare,' for 'he dare not', and so forth.

'The next to the last,' for 'the last but one,' is one of the commonest of phrases. As plurals we get *nesties* (nests), *postes* or *posties* (posts), etc., to any extent. *Baint* (or beent), for 'is not' still survives here and there, though it is evidently dying out. *To* after *help* is omitted, – 'She won't help carry the basket.' 'Directly minute' for 'immediately' is a curious phrase which may be heard used even by well-educated people of the upper middle class. 'Beleft' is the past participle of *believe*. Then people 'keep all on' doing things, and boys may be heard constantly using, 'No, you never,' 'No, I never,' and so on, for 'No, you did not,' 'No, I did not.'

The rustic Kentishman has a fairly copious vocabulary, and some of the words he uses are very curious ones. A very familiar word is 'flead', which Pegge defines as 'lard, or rather the leaf of fat whence lard is got.' To a native of the county it seems incredible that there should be millions of folk in England who never heard of either 'flead' or 'flead cakes'. 'Lodge' means a wood or toolshed, just about the last place where one would like to lodge. *Oast* or *oast-house* is so common a feature of the Kentish hop districts that the inhabitants look upon the word as inseparably connected with hops. Yet *oast* was used in Kent for a kiln long before hop culture was introduced. There were 'brick-oasts', or 'brickhosts', 'lymostes' (lime-oasts), and probably other species as well. A

THE PEA PICKERS

very short and handy word is 'lew', which is much better than the ordinary English 'sheltered'. 'It lays lew,' it lies in a sheltered position. Culverkeys, colverkeys, or cauverkeys is Kentish for cowslips, though a native of Charing called these flowers 'horsebuckles'. The word *shires*, pronounced *sheeres*, is used in a vague way to denote any part of England more than a county or two away. 'He comes from the sheeres,' or 'he's gone to live somewhere in the sheeres,' seems delightfully vague in a country possessing forty shires, but it seems to satisfy the good folks of rural Kent.

A very extraordinary expression is 'to make old bones', for to live to old age. To *make bones* at all seems a difficult matter, but to make *old* bones seems a truly puzzling feat. Yet the phrase is found all over Kent and some of the neighbouring counties. 'Kentish fire', for long and hearty cheering, is so well known that it need not be dwelt upon. Effect for *newt, crock*, a large earthenware pan or dish, *maybug* for *cockchafer, cater*, for *aslant* or *askew*, with scores of others are good Kentish words. *Nailbourne* or *eylebourne*, deserves a passing word. It signifies an intermittent brook, of which many exist in the county. Similar springs are met with in or near the Yorkshire Wolds, and are called *gipseys* (g hard, as in go). *Lathe* for a division of the county, and *Minnis*, a common (e.g. Stelling Minnis) seem

peculiar to this part of England. A *teg* (or *tag*) is a sheep of a year old; a hurdle is called a *wattle*. *Ampery*, mouldy, decayed, and *tetter*, cross, peevish, are very common. *Terrible*, often pronounced ter'bl, is almost invariably the word used to intensify the meaning. 'He's ter'bl bad,' 'dat aint ter'bl loikly,' 'dere's a ter'bl many rabbits 'bout here.' 'There's no bounds to him,' means 'there's no saying what he may do.'

One might go on culling these interesting words and phrases from the Kentish glossaries to almost any extent. Dip where you will into them, and you can hardly fail to light upon some racy old word or form of speech which 'bygone' Kentishmen used, but which, alas! is now either wholly obsolete, or on the way to becoming so. How many nowadays, especially of town-dwellers, would understand such a sentence as this given by Lewis: – 'I took up the libbit that lay by the soal, and hove it at the hagister that was in the poddergrotten?' I took up the stick that was lying by the pond, and threw it at the magpie that was in the pease-stubble. Yet *libbet, soal, hagister, podder* (peas, beans, etc.) *grotten* or *gratten* (stubble) were formerly good Kentish words, if they are now all forgotten in many parts of the country.

A glance at some of the old Kentish proverbs or proverbial sayings given by Pegge must conclude this imperfect paper:

73

HARBOUR AND BARRACKS, DOVER

THE OLD HOP PICKER

A knight of Cales,
A gentleman of Wales,
And a Laird of the North Countree;
A yeoman of Kent
With his yearly Rent,
Will buy 'em out all three.

This is one of the best known of these proverbial sayings. Learned men have disputed as to the origin of the curious phrase 'Neither in Kent nor Christendom.' Dover figures in a good many of these old sayings. 'Dover a den of thieves,' is as uncomplimentary to that town as

When it's dark in Dover
It's dark all the world over,

is the reverse. 'As sure as there's a dog in Dover' is at any rate more picturesque than the common 'as sure as a gun'. 'From Barwick (Berwick) to Dover' is equivalent to saying 'from one end of the land to the other.' Further uncomplimentary references to towns are found in such sayings as

Long, lazy, lousy Lewisham.

He that will not live long,
Let him dwell at Murston, Tenham, or Tong.

Folkestone – Kent Fools' is an anagram.

SANDWICH

He that rideth into the Hundred of Hoo,
Besides pilfering Seamen, shall find Dirt enow.

Deal Savage, Canterbury Parrots,
Dover Sharps, and Sandwich Carrots.

Naughty Ashford, surly Wye,
Poor Kennington hard by.

Richard Stead

WICKHAMBREAUX

In the region of Ickham and Wickham, there is an old countryside rhyme, as follows:

> Ickham, pickham
> Penny Wickham
> Cockalorum jay
> Eggs, butter, cheese, bread
> Hick, stick, stone dead!

Anon

WICKHAMBREAUX MILL

A CATCH OF SPRATS

'POOR, DEAR HEARTS'

To work hard for weeks on end without a penny wages is, unfortunately, the lot of many a Cinque Ports fisherman. His pay depends entirely upon his share of the amount the catch realizès.

Only a small number of them own boats. The others work, or assist the owner to work, for an agreed share of the profits. Some boats may be fitted with motors, but the majority depend on sail or oars; and the fishing ground lies in the track of the busiest shipping route in the world – the English Channel.

Some idea of the heart-breaking nature of the work and the insignificance of the profits can be formed from the following instance.

Starting out overnight, and owing to a motor breakdown not arriving ashore until the following afternoon, three fishermen landed a catch of sprats. As there were no buyers in the market they decided to hawk their catch in the streets at three-halfpence a pound. At five o'clock the police informed them that wet fish could not be sold in the streets after that hour. There was nothing else to do but wait for the next morning's market when their 11 stone of sprats fetched fivepence a stone. Fivepence for fourteen pounds which works out at 4s. 7d. to be divided among three men for a total of seventy-two hours' work!

No wonder the local nickname for a fisherman is 'Poor, Dear Heart'!

Frank Watts

HOPS AND HOP-PICKERS

Two or three weeks before the commencement of the picking, the exact date of which they had no means of ascertaining, thousands of poor persons overran the county of Kent, sleeping in the tramp wards of the union-houses or in the open air, and in the day time going round the country in search of employment. The inhabitants of the villages to which they went showed no sympathy towards a class of persons whose filthy, indecent, and disorderly habits made them unfit to be taken into their cottages, and who before the time of picking lived mainly by their depredations. The effect of this influx of strangers upon the resident population was grievously complained of; and when the hop-picking was over and the vast population was paid off to return to their homes, the scenes of debauchery and riot were described as frightful. Still worse was the state of things if, as not unfrequently occurs in the hop garden, a strike took place for an increase of remuneration, or some petty offence gave rise to a pitched battle between the immigrants and the natives.

'It is not to be supposed,' Mr Stanhope continues, 'that all hop-growers looked on at this state of things without attempting to remedy it. The efforts made, however, were very partial in their operation, and it was not until it had reached its climax that the public opinion of the county was fully roused, and it was determined to make an endeavour to remove the reproach which rested upon it in respect of the accommodation given to this population, and to devise some means by which the class of pickers might be improved and more control over them obtained by the planters. But only in 1866 was

HOP PICKERS

any united action taken, in which year the Society for the Employment and Improved Lodging of hop-pickers was formed by the adhesion of the principle hop-growers of the county, and by the support of many of the landowners. . . . One of its objects was to establish a system of engaging them by means of respectable and trustworthy agents living in the town from whence they came. The religious aspect of the question − how best to provide for the spiritual wants of this immigrant population − was designedly omitted, to prevent any chance of thereby alienating any of the planters.

'The class of persons employed in hop-picking varies according to the mode of hiring. In East Kent a class of pickers more akin to the home dwellers is to be found in those who come from the seaport towns or from Sussex villages, bringing with them furniture, beds, and cooking utensils. They are superior to the ordinary immigrants, and the inhabitants of the hop-growing villages are often not unwilling to receive them into their homes. They are not unfrequently hired through an agent in each town. In the neighbourhood of Maidstone, many pickers are also hired through the agency of the binmen or "gangers". A man living in London or the suburbs agrees beforehand with the planter by letter to bring down one or more "bins'" companies, from six to eight persons each, beside children. Generally each picker is paid separately for his or her work, but sometimes a system analogous to that of the public gang is adopted, and the ganger brings down his party to the scene of action, paying all expenses, feeding them mis-

erably, and giving them pehaps a trifling sum at the finish. Sometimes a costermonger takes them all down in his cart, feeds them, and gives them fixed wages, taking for himself the rest of the profits. In other cases also, even where each individual is paid what he or she had earned, extortions by these binmen are represented as by no means uncommon, and at any rate some treating or remuneration is expected by them in return for their services in collecting the party. This system appears on the whole to work fairly well, if the grower carries out his engagement. Sometimes, however, when the hops go off suddenly and the planter finds himself in no want of hands to pick them, he is careless about giving notice to them not to come, and in one case no less than one hundred pickers, arriving from London in accordance with their contract, found themselves thrown upon the road without employment or money.

'The most objectionable mode of hiring is that already mentioned of collecting them from the roads or from the tramp wards of the union-houses. It is no uncommon thing for a grower to send up at night to the union and to hire all who are to be found there, without any reference to decent behaviour or ability to perform the work. This system has been described as a direct premium on vagrancy, and is a very great hardship to the respectable poor who have to leave London without any certainty of employment.'

J. Y. Stratton

'BURNING OFF'

HOMEWARD BOUND

SOWING CORN

There is one old-fashioned farming operation, old since afore Noah was a sailor, which you may still see performed in the ancient manner in the country around the North Downs, and indeed most parts of Kent – sowing corn by hand from a basket slung from the shoulders, just as the farmer is doing it in Caldecott's *House that Jack Built* picture book. And the sickle still survives, in the guise of the 'bagging-hook', used for cutting grass and herbage on roadsides, and is sometimes employed in a badly rain and wind-laid cornfield. Most farming folk call it a 'rippuk', i.e. 'reap-hook'. We have been told that the flail is still occasionally used for threshing beans at Kentish farms, instead of the threshing-machine.

The old stumpy English sheep-dog of the Downs never seems to jump up barking at horse's noses, which is a favourite trick of the collie; perhaps it is a wolfish trait still persisting, for collies are reckoned snappy and of uncertain temper. Shakespeare was no doubt fond of dogs, but Crab is held up to us as a warning against spoiling dogs, as Launce did, and all

78

HEDGING

townsfolk do, whether they remain in town or rush out to farm in the country, with no farming knowledge. There are many such now amongst the North Down country, probably outnumbering the real villagers, who still speak good Kentish dialect and use good old English words. Should you ask a genuine villager for a road direction he will still generally use the term 'three' or 'four-went way', instead of the incorrect expression 'four cross roads', which in fact are only two cross roads with four directions to choose whither you will wend your way. The upstart and the original villagers possess one trick in common, in that neither can converse without over-working the questioning 'eh?', the newcomers do this because they are poor and unobservant listeners, the genuine villagers do this because it gives them time to consider before they reply; for most villagers are naturally and quite unconsciously suspicious – perhaps a legacy from feudal times. But with nei-ther party, as a rule, is this habit due to deafness, because after ejaculating 'eh?' and pausing, they usually reply to the ques-tion before it has to be reiterated. But the real villagers behave just in the same way amongst themselves as with strangers:

SMALLBROOKE, SPELDHURST

79

OUTSIDE BOYER'S PHOTOGRAPHIC ROOMS, SANDWICH

TWO COUNTRYWOMEN

We're joost th'sem among oursen;
When Missis barls out 'John!'
Ah nivver answer 'er joost then
But think — now what's she wan?
'John!' Doos she want th' chimbly swep?
There's nought amiss ah knows on,
Maybe she's fell dahn backdoor step;
She can barl out — joost 'ark yon!
There's allus summat what's amiss:
She's foun' yon broken coop:
Ah'll say it out — she's mad, she his,
'John!' Yis, well now, what's oop?
Ye can't like be too keerful:
If ast 'Be your name Gee?'
Nivver say aye nor nay
But 'I believe it be.'
An' when ye wish to speak ill
Don't say it straightaway
But 'I hear tell' or better still
Joost shoove it on 'they say.'
If mester offers ye a glass,
Don't answer 'aye' outright —
But mek it his obligement by
'Dunno but as I might.'
If y'ave no doubt a thing be so
Say 'Well, I doubt it be;'
It leaves ye freer like, ye know,
To chop and change, d'ye see?

80

BILSINGTON

SERVANT SWEEPING WITH A BESOM

GARDENER CUTTING WOOD

PENSHURST

When you seek a road direction from a villager, involving right and left hand turnings, make sure, if possible, what he really means. You meet him coming towards you, and he says, 'turn to the right when you get to owd Jimmy Smith's farm.' But he means right as he stands facing you; when you get to 'owd Jimmy Smith's farm' it will by your left, really. Perhaps it won't matter, though, as you will not know which of two or three farms is 'Jimmy Smith's'. In nine cases out of ten the villager will direct you wrongly. The titheman will rise to fame, sooner or later, and would without any extraneous and expensive help from school-boards. Seeing you are a stranger, he will say, 'The new tin shanty where it says on a board, "Broody hens and cabbages for sale".' Since the war many of the old guide-posts have rotted away or otherwise disappeared, and what signs remain are ugly iron things bearing cryptic hieroglyphics which may be meant for motor people, but if so they ignore them. But let us get the old guide-posts back, so long as they are not enamelled iron things made by M'Pherson & Lloyd of Birmingham, but genuine locals by the village carpenter; for these often combined instruction with humour.

Charles G. Harper and J.C. Kershaw

A BID FOR COTTAGE FURNITURE

A little below the inn, on the opposite side of the way, is a pollarded oak, and that leads beneath a couple of old cottages into the church-yard, through which there is a path to the great house. The cottages form a sort of archway, and are very fine specimens of the timbered building which was in vogue before lath and plaster played the important part they now do in modern dwellings. From the churchyard their appearance is particularly striking. They form a fit introduction to the old church and 'castle', and I was glad to hear that Lord de L'Isle would 'not have them taken down for any money'. He has, indeed, been at considerable expense to keep them in repair – only a small part of the very heavy drain which this estate must have kept up on his purse. Near the door of one of these cottages I noticed an old-fashioned piece of furniture, and begged to be allowed to look at it. It was of oak, curiously carved, and black with age – a sort of cabinet or sideboard. The woman with the keys said it belonged to her husband's family; that the owner had been offered £5 and even £7 for it by 'a person as came from London', but that he would not sell it because it 'had been such a long time in the family'. I could

LENHAM

not help thinking that it was much to the cottager's credit to keep his heirloom, and resist the temptations of that crafty person 'as came from London'.

The day before my visit (2nd October 1876) there had been 'harvest services' in the church, and the decorations were not yet withered. Round the entrance door was a garland of yellow hops, and the pillars inside were adorned with the bloom of the same plant, intertwined with chrysanthemums and other autumn flowers. There was a wreath of apples near the reading desk, bright rose-cheeked apples, with a great branch of the 'crab' near them, and various specimens of the harvest of the district. This is one of the good old simple customs which is still preserved in many parts of the country, and which it is hoped will survive the 'march of improvement' yet a little longer.

Louis J. Jennings

PUDDING-PIES

Pudding-Pies, both the name and manufacture of these delicacies are peculiar to the County of Kent, it was customary to eat them during Lent. The fashion of going Pudding-Pieing, on the Lenten Sundays, was to take a walk to some village Alehouse and there to partake of Pudding-Pies and Ale. The origin of this quaint custom is lost in obscurity.

Edwin Harris

THE 'BOY'

A rude little boy stationed himself in front of the camera at Lenham, with a view of becoming the most conspicuous portion of our picture of the quaint market-place. He was unaware of the resources of photography. We 'exposed' without drawing the slide. The urchin was circumvented by this ruse, and ran off bursting with pride and glee to tell his mates that he had been photographed. Meanwhile, the slide cover was withdrawn, and a negative secured. Just outside one of the old half-timber houses, behind the colonnade of poplars, a man and a dog had posed themselves. We were glad that neither of these (and especially the dog) was deceived by our stratagem. Within limits, we appreciate the addition of portraits of local celebrities, as they add interest and authenticity to our pictures. The sagacity of the dog formed an excuse for Higgins to relate a few anecdotes. But dog stories are so much overdone, that his imaginative efforts fell rather flat.

As a rule the dog is one of the least intelligent of animals – certainly he fails entirely in comparison with the cat or the raven. He is docile and tractable, readily learning by heart any trick, if there is any reward promised. It need not necessarily be edible. A piece of wood or a stone will usually serve as effectual a temptation as a biscuit. If you are at table he is, of course, disappointed to find that he cannot chaw up or extract nourishment from the piece of boxwood for which you have required him to shake hands or beg; but he will soon return to the charge.

NEAR BIDDENDEN

The leading characteristic of the dog is the unchangeable persistence with which he will pursue some fixed idea. Like a systematic gambler, he backs that idea, regardless of repeated failure, introducing it on every possible occasion, knowing that the right concordance of circumstances must eventually come according to the rules of chance, when that mode of action will turn out trumps.

My dog at home bites every stranger who ventures into the back-yard; no doubt with a vague idea that if he causes one trespasser to repent, there will be joy enough in my household to cover all the displeasure at the ninety and nine just persons who have to retreat hurriedly to the nearest chemist. Some collateral ancestor of this dog dwelt in some open prairie, where the grass was coarse and stiff: my dog obstinately continues to turn round three times whenever he wishes to repose on the soft, thick Turkey rug in front of the drawing-room fire.

H. Parr

CHARLES DICKENS AS I KNEW HIM

As for Dickens himself, the weather very seldom kept him from the pedestrian exercises, of which he was so fond; and many a misty walk we took to the marshes at Cooling, that we might get a realistic notion of the dreariness and loneliness of the scenes in *Great Expectations*, made famous by 'Pip' and the convict. On such occasions as these we not unfrequently returned wetted to the skin by a drenching rain.

One of the most delightful days of this visit was occupied by a drive from Gad's Hill to Canterbury, a distance of twenty-nine miles, over the old Dover Road, through Rochester, Chatham, Sittingbourne and Faversham.

We were to make an early start, so as to give plenty of time for luncheon, in a beautiful spot already chosen, and allow for a ramble afterwards.

Two post carriages were turned out with postilions, in the red jackets of the old Royal Dover Road, buck-skin breeches, and top-boots into the bargain.

PILGRIMAGE TO CANTERBURY

The preparations for this new pilgrimage to Canterbury were of the most lavish description, and I can see now the hampers and wine baskets blocking the steps of the house before they were packed in the carriages.

Everyone was in the best of spirits, the weather was all that could be desired, and the ladies did honour to it by the brightness of their costumes. We were all glad, too, that the restoration of the Chief's health enabled him to enjoy as much pleasure himself as he was giving to his friends.

We started sharp to time, and travelled merrily over the road, with hop-gardens on either side, until we reached Rochester, our horses making such a clatter in this slumbrous old city that all the shop-keepers in the main street turned out to see us pass.

Mr Dickens rode in the foremost carriage, and having occasion to pull up at the shop of one of the tradesmen in the main street of Rochester, a small crowd collected round the carriages. It seemed to be pretty generally known amongst them that Dickens was of the party, and we got a good deal of fun out of the mistake made by a man in the crowd, who pointed up at Mr James T. Fields, and called out, 'That's Dickens!' Poor Fields was in great confusion, especially when Mr Dickens, to complete the deception, handed up a small parcel to him, with the request, 'Here you are, Dickens, take charge of this for me.'

Away we went again through Rochester, and skirting Chatham, were soon again in the open country on the road to Sittingbourne, where a relay of horses was awaiting us.

A short rest in the brick-making town was quite sufficient for us, and we sped on to that haven of rest where it had been arranged that we should lunch. A more suitable spot could not have been found. It lay in the deep shades of a wood, with a rippling stream running through.

The breakfast hour had been an early one, and the long drive had given an excellent edge to our appetites. We turned to with a ready will to unload the carriages, and carry the baskets into the wood. Everybody did something, and the cloth was speedily laid. An hour was the time allowed for luncheon, and out of this we had to let the postilions get their meal when we had finished. Dickens would not let us start again until every vestige of our visit to the wood in the shape of lobster shells and other debris, had been removed.

There was never a more delightful ride on a summer's evening than the one we took then. The day was fast closing in, and as there was no reason for loitering on the road, we sped along at a rattling pace.

The journey from Gad's Hill to Canterbury had taken nearly five hours, including the time allowed for luncheon and loitering. The journey home was made in less than three, and we forgot our fatigue in the enjoyment of supper. It seems to me,

ON THE HILLS NEAR SNODLAND

CANTERBURY

as I look back over the years that have intervened, that I enjoyed a great privilege, no less than a rare pleasure in being in the company of my dear old Chief when he took this his last visit to Canterbury, in the streets of which he had so often wandered in his earlier days. . . .

Walter Dexter

THE DOWNS AND THE GOODWIN SANDS

At the present moment the remains of a large steamer is to be seen, humped, with a broken hull, on the Goodwins. This is the four-masted passenger steamer *Mahratta*, nearly 4,000 tons, and belonged to the Brocklebank line. She was homeward bound from India to London, carrying passengers and a general cargo, consisting chiefly of rubber, rice, tea, and jute. The vessel seems to have got out of her course on Thursday, April 8th, 1909, and struck the part of the sands known as Fawk Spit. 'On the following day, which was Good Friday, lifeboats were launched, but the steamer was found to be hard on the sands.' Two of the most powerful tugs obtainable were sent from Dover, and other tugs attended the ship, but it was impossible to drag her afloat. The passengers were landed at Deal pier by the lifeboat. All the boatmen of Deal were engaged to transfer baggage and jettison cargo in order to lighten the ship.

The passengers included two families with women and children.

THE WRECK OF THE *MAHRATTA*

On Saturday night the ship broke in two. The engineer officer, Mr J. Matthews, says the ship was strained, and there was a continual grinding and snapping as plates sheered and buckled and heavy iron rivets broke away by dozens. The crew and the boatmen from shore were salving tea and throwing jute overboard. Men were working up to the knees in water. Suddenly the ship broke with a sound like that of a cannon, breaking across the bunkers and saloon. 'One labourer was so scared he caught hold of me round the body and I found it hard to get clear from him. Steam was shut off as the water was rising rapidly in the engine-room and an explosion was feared. The water in the engine-room was up to our waists when we went down there.'

The chief engineer on finding the ship on the sands committed suicide by cutting his throat.

Three passengers were on board when the ship broke, including a lady, who had declined to go ashore because her dog would have had to stay six months under veterinary supervision. The crew of ninety and one hundred boatmen and labourers from Deal and the neighbourhood were also there.

A strong westerly wind and a heavy sea soon began to damage the ship, as it lay right on the sands in shallow water – a position rendering salvage operations difficult. The salvage steamer *Cheshire* was used to take rice and jute out of Nos 4 and 5 holds. As the vessel sank and listed over further, salvage grew more and more difficult.

The following paragraph in the *Times* of April 27th may be worth reproducing:

A Deal hawker's cart which was stopped in Dover was found to contain two chests of tea, weighing 170 lb, from the wrecked liner *Mahratta*. The man . . . said he found the tea on the Deal sand hills. He was charged yesterday with having shipwrecked goods in his possession and with the intention to defraud the Customs. He was fined £9 5s., including costs, with the alternative of a month's imprisonment.

The running of a ship right on to the Goodwins in calm weather is so unusual that it may be of interest to know how the accident occurred. The Board of Trade inquiry at Liverpool found that the pilot had failed to recognise the Gull light when he first saw it and in consequence had taken a wrong course. The second mate and the pilot, it was held, ought to have called the master, who was not then on duty, at the time when the second mate reported the light to the pilot and the pilot failed to recognise it.

★ I am indebted for certain particulars to *Heroes of the Goodwins*, by the Rev. T.S. Treanor.

Arthur D. Lewis

NEAR BENENDEN

COTTAGE GARDENS

When we return from visiting other lands, we notice with grateful eyes these wayside homely gardens, which are peculiarly English. Englishmen have always loved their gardens, and all classes share in this affection. It is not so with other European nations. You do not find abroad those flowers in cottage windows cherished so carefully through the winter months; you do not see the thrifty Frenchman or German stealing from his potato ground or onion bed a nice broad space for the cultivation of flowers. Whereas in England you will scarcely find a cottage garden that is not gay and bright with beautiful flowers, or the poorest labourer, however large his family may be, willing to sacrifice the plants in which he takes so great a pride.

At all seasons of the year these cottage gardens look beautiful. Snowdrops and crocuses seem to rear their heads earlier in the springtime in their village plots than in the gardens of the great. Yellow and purple crocuses are there, and then a little later dog-violets, and yellow daffodils. My villagers have given me bunches of violets long before they grew in the rectory garden, save those Neapolitan ones that flourish in a frame.

Primroses transplanted from the neighbouring woods are not despised. A few stray tulips begin to show themselves, immensely prized by the cottager, and soon the wallflowers are in bloom filling the air with beautiful scent, and for-get-me-nots reflect the blueness of the sky. Villagers love the simple polyanthus, and soon on the wall of the cottage is seen the red japonica in full flower. Then the roses come into bloom, and many a cottage can boast of its fine Floire de Dijon or Marechal Niel or strong-growing crimson rambler. Clematis plants of various hues are seen on many a cottage wall, and ivy 'that creepeth o'er ruins old' loves to cling to rustic dwelling-places, and sometimes clothes walls and thatch and chimney with its dark green leaves. The honeysuckle is a favourite plant for climbing purposes. It covers the porch and sheds its rich perfume around, nor in the warmer parts of England is the vine unknown.

The southern counties of England afford the most luxuriant examples of cottage gardens which form a conspicuous charm of our villages.

P.H. Ditchfield

HOP OASTS, BARMING

HOP-OASTS

The village is beautifully situated, sheltered by the steep folds of the hills behind it. Hop-oasts cluster here and there, and peer above hedgerows and coppices, sometimes oddly like strange giraffe-like animals with questing heads. Get an oast-house in a certain light, and in a particular silhouetted grouping, and it looks with its leaning cowl and projecting wind-vane a very weird thing indeed.

Charles G. Harper and J.C. Kershaw

OLD KENT COUNTY C.C.

The following advertisement appeared in *Bells Life* and the *Sporting Life* of 1872.

The Old Kent County C.C.

> Three old players of the above club and natives of the celebrated parish of Benenden, Mr T.G. Wenmen (age 71), Mr E.G. Wenmen (age 71) and Mr R. Mills (age 77) take the liberty of giving a public challenge to play a match of cricket with any three of England of not less than 73. They will make the match for any amount not exceeding £100.

The challenge was not taken up.

A.F. Abell

KENTISH CRICKETER

STONE, ISLE OF OXNEY

THE LONELY ROAD

The ten miles of road from Guldeford to Lydd is the loneliest on the Marsh. For half the way it is the only one that traverses this six-mile belt of solitude, since for lanes and cross-roads there is here no need. It bends and twists at times before the frequent obstacles of a bedyked country, or again for a mile it romps away in a straight line to be suddenly brought up short to an uncompromising right angle and forced once more into a devious course. It is a little sad in winter, but then it ought to be or it wouldn't be the Marsh! The dark water ruffles coldly in the full dykes beside the road, the flowering reeds that whisper soothingly along their fringes in summer days rattle their dead stems together like dry bones in the winter wind. Here and there a row of giant willows, their warped trunks bulging beneath the surface of some brimming stream, strikes a note of contrast in the foreground of this wide waste. The moorhens, which in summer mock at you with raucous note, from their safe harbourage of reed or alder, of willow bush or briar, are now surprised in the open and dash for safety on nimble feet or fluttering wing. The green pastures are everywhere patched with the tawny hue of the withered summer herbage. The sheep are no longer white but carry fleeces almost as dark from the salt sea mists as those of the smoke-stained specimens that roam the London Parks. The peewit too is everywhere abroad; that really cheerful and not unsociable bird, who in spite of himself gives forth a cry more calculated than almost any wild-bird note to announce the pathos of the waste, be it moor or marsh, mountain or downland. Seagulls always gregarious, whether upon the earth or in the air, scream in discordant chorus far away. A 'looker' will probably be somewhere within sight, his shaggy dogs working in the leisurely manner that a flat country, heavy sheep and comparatively small enclosures permit. Indeed the dogs hereabouts have an easy time, save in very hard weather when the dykes freeze and the sheep range over the whole country. They do not run their hearts to a standstill in six or seven years like the collies of North Wales and Cumberland.

A.G. Bradley

HEARTHS AND HOMES

The peasant housewife is a very kind and gracious body, sturdy and independent, who will welcome you with all the graces of a duchess to her humble dwelling; but if you are foolish, superior and patronising, and, still worse, very curious, the cottage door will perhaps be shut when next you are pleased to call, and you will not be able to buy 'for an old song' those charming pieces of Staffordshire ware wrought in curious figures, nor add to your collection of old furniture that delightful little escritoire that had been in the cottager's family for years. True it was very battered and worm-eaten; but it could be easily renovated. However, it is no good – you will not get it. You

WASHERWOMEN

have offended the old lady by your behaviour, and all the king's horses and all the king's men will not force her to part with her treasures to you. In future it is well to remember that poor people have feelings, very proper feelings, and good manners too, and to ride roughshod over them is not altogether wise, prudent, or seemly.

The old dame who welcomes you at the door has reached the autumntide of life. 'It is toward evening and the day is far spent.' She has brought up a large family, who have started well in life and are doing well. She has known what hard work meant, when she helped her husband to earn money to bring up the children by herself working in the fields. These rustic women are a fine race. They have often very tender souls in coarse bodies, wide, weather-reddened faces, not ill to look upon, calm, passive and veracious as the fields. It is hard work trimming swedes for sheep, picking up potatoes, going among the mangolds with skirts and sleeves sopping wet, the muddy soil clinging to everything. It is hard work, but it has its compensations. The air is bracing and health-giving. Passing one's days in the open air beneath the broad sky, witnessing the constant changes, the warm sunshine of the hayfield, the stern desolation of miles of snow, life becomes a very real thing. Hysteria and sentimentalism cannot live in such an atmosphere; and our friend could tell us that she has never had time for such nonsense. She has had troubles – very great they have been, and would have crushed many who have not been brought up in her school. But she has triumphed over them, or rather borne

them very bravely, and she is a real picture of a peasant woman, not one of those feeble caricatures which artists love to paint of lamblike old imbeciles with snowy caps and amiable smiles which are supposed to represent our peasant women.

Her husband, too, is a fine specimen of an old labourer. He can tell you many stories of the past life of the village, of hungry times of the Crimean War, when wages were low, when bread was two shillings a gallon, when he scarcely knew the taste of meat, and he was half starved and his father could not provide loaves enough for the family. He can remember the times of agitation and feverish unrest, when men's passions were aroused, and crowds of angry rustics scoured the country breaking the new-fangled machines which they imagined would take the bread out of the mouths of their wives and children. Those were the days of rick-firing, and he remembers seeing many a farmstead blazing, many a home made desolate by the blind fury of an enraged people. He can tell you of the old popular belief in the power of witches and of the 'evil eye', and of the 'wise men' who could counteract their evil influence, discover tools that had been lost or stolen. His back is bowed and he suffers severely from rheumatism; but he is very patient. As old age comes on it seems to bring with it a child-like piety which enables him to face death unmoved and to bear suffering with unmurmuring patience.

P.H. Ditchfield

91

THE CROSSROADS

'NO!' WAS THE ANSWER

In one of my walks from Tunbridge Wells, through the village of Ashurst, having occasion to stop at a small public-house, I met with a labouring man somewhat excited from having drank a little too much. He was, however, very communicative, which answered well my purpose. I said, after insinuating myself into his good graces.

'Can you read or write?'

'No!' was the answer.

'Do you ever go to church?'

'No!'

I replied, 'You wrong yourself in not going there.'

He said, 'Our parson once had fifty pounds to give away, and I got none of it, and that is the reason I never intend to go to church again.'

I said, 'You must forgive your enemies, if you wish to inherit eternal life, and receive pardon for all the sins you have committed.' I remarked that the Bible laid down those principles of religious doctrine in the most positive and undoubted manner.

He remarked, 'If you say so, you, I'm sure, are no scholar, for I'm sure that 'aint never in the Bible.'

Such was his mental, moral and religious condition. Let us now see to his physical state. He had not had a comb in his hair for a year, and confessed that he did not wash his hands and face every morning. The Lord's Prayer, Belief, and other parts of the Catechism, were as foreign to his nature, practice, and principles, as the American continent is distant from the village in which he lived.

J. Shaw

WIND AND WATER

Were it not that the term huffling was in vogue before Lewis Carroll invented the portmanteau word, we might have explained its origin by saying that it was meant to denote a combination of hurrying and scuffling. It is certainly an expressive word. It is a still more exciting occupation. The manoeuvring of a sailing barge, lowering her mast as she negotiates the bridge, and then getting all her tackle up again, if possible, without having to anchor – this is the work of a huffler, or bridge-pilot. In the London river a pilot must be licensed, but in the Swale and Medway, at King's Ferry and Rochester, it is a case of the survival of the fittest. Any of us could take a boat and cadge for a job, but I don't think we

THE BARGEMAN

should be at it long. It is quite easy to get killed or to lose a mast by any of a hundred and one errors of judgment. For a barge to engage a huffler is practically compulsory, because the insurance companies would repudiate a claim for accident made by a skipper who had taken the bridge without assistance.

The huffler waits in his boat about half a mile from the bridge. He boards his barge – you can always tell a barge with a huffler on board by the two boats in tow – takes charge, for he is now responsible, and, with the skipper and mate assisting, gets the tackle ready for lowering away. With a following wind it is simple to lower and get up tackle again without risk of getting stuck or having to anchor, but the niceties of huffling are to be seen when the barge is tacking; the wind blowing from the direction of the bridge she is approaching. A tack to the side of the river, then she goes about and makes a short tack to the central arch. Then, when perilously near the bridge, she lowers away, dives into the teeth of the wind, and passes under the arch. As soon as she is through, her helm is put over to keep her at an angle to catch the wind again, and all hands strenuously work at the winch, her heavy canvas flapping noisily and everything, apparently, at sixes and sevens. With luck she will have her mast sufficiently raised to go about before reaching the shallows of the bank, and then get off in proper trim. Sometimes her foresail is gathered up on the stay before lowering. Sometimes, however, when the wind is light she will duck her canvas with foresail still spread to give her the maximum sail area.

MAIDSTONE WHARF

SMALLHYTHE

I have known a barge dismasted owing to a gust of wind filling her sail at the last moment of lowering, so that her mast would not budge. In bad weather it is often a dangerous game, and men have been killed through tackle breaking. On the whole, however, it is amazing how few accidents happen. At times, in windy weather, you can see half a dozen barges flopping about the river like wounded birds, and at night there seems to the onlooker on shore to be a scene of indescribable confusion, yet they will sort themselves out in a few minutes and proceed on their journey as if bridges were things that had never entered into their calculations – thanks to the huffler.

This exciting manoeuvre of getting down tackle and up again, if possible without dropping anchor, can be witnessed in a lesser degree at King's Ferry bridge, near Queenborough, but the strong tides of the Medway give an extra zest to the huffler's art in Rochester.

Barges with their picturesque lines and pleasing colouring seem to show no signs of being displaced by modern progress. The sailing ship may become a thing of the past, but the sailing barge, on account of its cheapness, will stay. It is amazing where they can go, handled by only two men, and sometimes by a man and a boy. In Holland, in Germany, in Belgium, and in France the traveller will see the familiar red sails of Thames and Medway barges. In old pictures of a hundred years ago the English sailing barge seemed to be almost identical with her successor of today except for the square sail, which was a feature of those times. It is probably the difficulty of handling this auxiliary that has led to its abandonment.

Probably in those days, when labour was cheaper, more hands were carried. Two men can negotiate almost any weather with a spritsail barge, because the mainsail is brailed as it stands, and the foresail and topsail come down with a run on letting go the halyard and cannot very well get into difficulties.

Donald Maxwell

THE PARISH CLERK

The parish clerk of the following paragraph was not a Sussex man, it is true, though he lived only a few miles across the Kentish border. It was, however, from a Sussex man, who was present in church at the time, that my informant, a Robertsbridge neighbour, got the story.

The old clerk set the hymns, managed the singing, and worked the barrel-organ. He was, however, so partial to the 'Old Hundredth', that in an evil hour the clergyman asked him if he could not now and then give them another tune, and if it wasn't on the barrel whether he couldn't set it with a pitch-pipe. The old man didn't say much at the time, but evidently felt deeply this interference with his authority as master of the music, and accordingly at the next singing he gave out –

'Let us sing to the praise and glory of God, the hundred and nineteenth psalm, from *eend to eend*' (176 verses).

John Coker Egerton

TONBRIDGE SCHOOL

THE COMING OF THE RAILWAY

The South-Eastern Railway got its Act in 1836, and the piece of line from Redhill to our town was not completed until 1842. In the interval Tonbridge (as I have heard from those who lived here at the time) was not a pleasant place of residence. The swarm of navvies which descended like locusts upon the place may have been welcomed by the keepers of the lesser public-houses and other undesirable resorts, but the ordinary resident prayed for the speedy completion of the railway. Drunkenness and fighting were of nightly occurrence, and a big tree which then stood in Botany Bay was a favourite rendezvous for these pugilistic encounters. So great a nuisance did these unfortunate men become, and so greatly were they disliked, that the word 'navvy' became a synonym for a person of low tastes and behaviour. Mr Rivington in his *History of Tonbridge School* says that in the 'forties, 'fifties and 'sixties of last century the word was applied in the School to every youth of the lower orders and that such youths were regarded as natural foes. It is true that class-feeling ran high and that 'town and gown' fights were not uncommon. But the use of the word navvy was not confined to the School, though it may have originated there. It was in more or less general use in the town as a term of opprobrium or reproach until the late eighties; but I have not heard it used for nearly forty years. The present generation of School boys knows it not.

A.H. Neve

THE JOY OF DIGGING

We are often ashamed of the Earth – the brown soggy clutch of it at our feet, the toil of it, the healthy, common ruggedness of it. To us, with our white linens and dainty ways, it seems coarse, a thing to be avoided. To one who lives for long on such a place as Romney Marsh this idea will soon become a matter to be laughed at. On the marsh the earth is the source of all things, and association with it is the renewal of life. Sheila Kaye-Smith speaks of the marsh earth as 'soft and rich and alive,' and this is the description of one who knows. To learn something of the real quality of the earth, one should be up and out on the marsh at five in the morning with a spade. It was my fortune to help a 'looker' to cut out a dyke at this hour, and it is an experience that I shall ever look back upon with satisfaction. I do not ever remember getting a fuller sixty seconds worth of emotion out of each minute in my life . . . the world had never been so generous to my senses. As I walked over Guldeford Level on that still morning all the world crowded to meet me. Fresh from sleep and with a palate untainted by food or drink, my sensitiveness to the odours of the marsh was acute. The air was heavy with the mist and the salt of the sea . . . and with it came a dozen suggestions – the scent of haws and blackberries, of dew-soaked grass, of wood smoke, of sheep, of the earth. The 'looker' and I came to the dyke, and we dug. We stood in the water of the dyke and chopped the weeds and scraped and drove our spades into the steaming earth. Every spadeful I took up was a benison. As I

'POPE'S GANG'

smacked the warm tufts on the bank they gave back to me the acrid smell of the marsh, and he who smells that aroma without digging for it is getting a poor second-hand thing. He is getting the ghost of an odour – the sun-tamed, jaded apology of the real thing.

For an hour I worked with the thrill of conquest running in me, but I was soon feeling hot and parched. My friend Fagge, the 'looker', set a tremendous pace and I could see he was eager to have me give in. However, I had determined to take my fair share in the digging and I went straight on with my spade. I stopped for a moment to discard my cardigan. Fagge's jaw was set like iron, and he went at his work as though the Wicked Men of Wittersham were at his muddy elbows. I did not think of anything. I dug not knowing, not caring, only taking joy in the pull of my muscles. After another thirty minutes I was going more slowly, and I felt the sun on my back. The spade was not cutting and swinging so easily, and every minute warned me that I should have to cease work. I stripped off my shirt, and went at it again for fifteen minutes. I became a machine – unthinking, mechanical. I blindly followed the music of Fagge's spade, keeping time to it with my own. Thrust down – out with the clod – up with it – and away with it – back again empty. It was now a hard, slow pull. I prayed that Fagge would soon stop for breakfast. I could no longer keep time with his spade. I was malingering, resting on my spade between my thrusts. Suddenly Mrs Fagge appeared on the bank.

'Harry!' she called, 'I reckon you two had better come up for bread-and-butters.'

Old Fagge stopped digging. I dropped my spade and climbed out of the ditch. Fagge followed me, and we walked back together to his cottage, where we found a great pot of tea and bread, butter, and bacon. I stopped at the pump and soused my head, dashed water on my arms and washed my hands. My body pleasantly tired, glowing, aching, tickled with the sweet smell of wood fire, gave me a dozen pleasant sensations as I sat down comfortably in a deep chair and stretched my legs. Oh, but it was fine! I had received the freedom of the earth – my clothes were covered with its ruddy brown crust from head to heel. Out of the earth I was moulded and into earth I shall return.

There is a great essay to be written on wielding a spade. I may not be able to write it . . . Anyhow I have lived it!

Standing on an oak table in one corner of Fagge's cottage I noticed a dozen mole pelts tacked down to boards. The 'lookers' on the marshes often make quite a considerable amount of money by trapping moles which are worth about sixpence each. The following is Fagge's method of skinning and drying the skins: Cut off the feet with a pair of scissors; cut the skin open straight down the centre of the belly and draw it off. Afterwards gently stretch it to a square shape, tack it, fur side down, to a board. Never dry skins in the sun or fire, but put them in a room with open windows and they will dry naturally, in a few days. Never put salt, alum, or chemical preservatives on the skins. Air drying is all that is necessary. Moles are in winter fur and best condition from the middle of December to the end of March, and should, therefore, be trapped during mid-winter to sell at best prices.

R. Thurston Hopkins

THE RIVER NEAR MAIDSTONE

THE LAND OF THE BRIDGES

A little more than a mile above the lock, Maidstone comes into sight – a poor approach, like the approach to most towns; but there is a good view ahead when the group of ancient river-side buildings appear at the bend above the town. The fourteenth-century Palace, All Saints' Church, and the College, which dates from 1260, made a magnificent group. The best view is obtained from the bridge, or, to be quite consistent the device-for-crossing-the-river-by-road.

Were it not for the knowledge of the country I have obtained at other times, I should have singularly little idea of the Medway between Maidstone and Wateringbury, for here it was that Brown left me to manage the boat alone. He had called for letters and found that he would have to run up to town for the day, but first he instructed me in the art of driving the engine. With cheery optimism I suggested meeting him in a few hours' time at Tonbridge. He, with less faith in my mechanical powers, delicately hinted that it was possible I might not get so far. Finally, we arranged that I should telegraph my position in the afternoon and he would join me wherever that should be.

He started the engine and hopped out, while I shot forward, confident of success. Brown watched me until the corner took me out of sight, looking, I thought, somewhat anxious; but I was sure there was no need to fear. He had told me exactly what to do in any emergency. I was not in the least disconcerted when the engine stopped as I was passing the wharves at Tovil. I started it again, just like Brown did, with great success and considerable surprise that it was so simple.

OLD COLLEGE GATE, MAIDSTONE

97

RIVERSIDE SCENE NEAR MAIDSTONE

I thought with some scorn of Brown's statement that the artistic temperament did not go with mechanical skill. Then it stopped again and I started it again – not, it is true, with quite the same facility; but still the engine was running, if somewhat spasmodically. I then did a fatal thing, as I found out afterwards. I increased the supply of petrol. With base ingratitude the thing stopped altogether, and refused to be coaxed into going at all.

Tying up the boat, I landed and sought professional advice. The only assistance I could get was from a man who assured me he understood everything about engines, having spent most of his life among them. By this time I had given up the attempt to find a motor-boat expert, so I accepted his offer. He began by asking where the fire was, which was not encouraging. He explained that all the engines he had ever managed had fires. I told him that the only fires we ever had on board were accidental; but he said he thought he could soon find out what was the matter. He looked at the motor and said it wanted oiling. Producing a can he pronounced it all right if it were once started. I tried immediately, and it went merrily. What a wonderful thing is expert knowledge! I thought half a crown had been too easily earned, but I was thankful that the boat was going so well. However, it soon began to fail again, and not far below East Farleigh Lock it stopped dead. This time I found a real engineer, or, at any rate, a man wearing a boiler suit, which inspired not a little confidence in the uninitiated. He started the engine at once, and I could not see in what way his starting differed from mine. But I suppose the engine could.

Now that the boat was going so well I did not want to stop it just because of a mere lock. Brown had shown me how to move the clutch and thus alter the angle of the propeller blades for stopping still or going astern. I therefore dashed into the lock at full speed and then reversed. Somehow the boat did not pull up as quickly as I had expected she would, and I charged the upper gates with considerable force.

There was a crash, and then I found the reversing business was being overdone, and I was rushing backwards out of the lower gates. I jammed on full speed ahead and made another wild plunge forward, churning up the water all around. I reversed sooner this time, and then settled down to a series of nerve racking spurts backwards and forwards, but managed to hit nothing. By this time I became dimly conscious of another boat, which had apparently broken adrift in the lock, and beheld an elderly lady climbing in terror up a slippery weed-covered ladder, shouting for help. Thus the promptings of humanity rather than faintheartedness in experimental motor-boating compelled me to stop the engine.

98

FISHING IN THE LOCK

RIVER MEDWAY

HOP PICKERS

When Brown responded to my telegram by joining me at the lock below Wateringbury, whither I had made my way by means of every device known to navigation, except motor-power, he explained what had been wrong in my management. I had turned on too much petrol. Consequently the valve soon froze. The work of the two alleged engineers was mere coincidence. In each case there had been an interval for liquefaction, and any one could have started the engine for a time, although it would obviously soon get into the same condition again. Under Brown's control, the boat ran without a hitch, and in about twenty minutes we were entering Yalding Lock.

Donald Maxwell

KENTISH SAYINGS

In the hop-districts of Kent, the fecundity of the Aphis is proverbial. A few only of these insects are sufficient to produce the disastrous hop-blight, by reason of their prodigious increase. Hence the saying in some parts of Kent – 'Two flies are enough to blight an acre of Goldings.'

'When England wrings, the Island sings.' This saying has special reference to Thanet. The island, as is well-known, is very productive, the soil being particularly fertile. Thanet may, therefore, be looked to for abundant crops when other parts of the country fall short.

D. Lee

SHAKESPEARE CLIFF, DOVER

THE KENT COAL-FIELDS

The Kent coal-fields represent an industry which, as yet, is in its infancy. Geologists have long believed that there was coal underlying a considerable portion of the County of Kent. On the suspension of the Channel Tunnel Works an opportunity occurred to test this theory. From the base of the Round Down Cliff, west of Dover, the Channel Tunnel Company sank a shaft down to the lower grey chalk, from the bottom of which they drove a heading 2,200 feet under the Straits of Dover. That stage having been reached in 1882, the Government caused the work to be suspended on national grounds, and while the company waited the final decision of Parliament as to whether the Channel Tunnel should be made or not, it was decided, on the advice of Professor Boyd Dawkins, to employ the men and machinery in exploring for coal. A boring was commenced in 1886, and in February, 1890, a seam of coal was reached at a depth of 1,190 feet. That first touch of the coal measures settled once for all that the theories of the geologists were accurate, but the actual value of the discovery had to be tested by further boring, for the first

seam, which was two feet six inches from top to bottom, with a parting in it of six inches of shale, was not, as far as could be judged, a very high class of fuel. The exploration was continued down to a depth of 2,221 feet, during which the boring tool cut through fourteen seams, representing an aggregate thickness of twenty-two feet of coal. Some of the seams are undoubtedly too thin to be workable, but nine of them might be worked, seven are two feet each or more, and the lowest four feet. When the boring was suspended they were still in the coal measures, and it is believed that there are other seams below. Such being the prospect they commenced sinking, and at present the shaft in which they cut the first seam has to be completed. After that, before much development can be done, the Coal Mining Acts will require that a second shaft should be carried down. These are operations which will require time and money, but beyond that, it has been now definitely proved that there is nothing to interfere with the development of a great coal-field in Kent, which will bring in its train many other industries.

T. Bavington Jones

101

GROVE FERRY

THE FERRY

The road to Harty undulates; the cliffs at Warden Point are to your right as you go back from Leysdown; a sombre green headland with wooded summit and a rust-red edge by the grey sea – so did it appear to me as I set out early – a white-washed farm with a red-tiled roof and a yellow haystack formed a group set up between me and the headland, and the heavy clouds, rimmed below with silver, cast shadows on the fields with their sheep and cattle. The isle is called Sheppey, it is said, because of its many sheep. The road goes near to the Swale – you see sails of barges rising out of the fields – and then turns and keeps inland, disappointing you, if it is new to you and you are impatient to cross. A boy with sheep going the opposite way to two men with cows was occasioning some difficulty on the narrow road as I passed. At last the Ferry Inn, a one-storied pale building, with a roof made green by lichen, over-looking the wide water, a mile across at high tide, of a brown colour. 'The man will be down directly,' said the land-lady. He was an old hand at the oar, and I crossed without the experiences of Mr Polly's passenger, who (if you remember *The History of Mr Polly*, by Wells) punting for the first time conveyed his passenger 'tortuously into the midst of a thicket of forget-me-not spangled sedges, splashed some water-weed over him, hit him twice with the punt pole, and finally landed him, alarmed but abusive, in treacherous soil at the edge of a hay meadow about forty miles down stream, where he imme-diately got into difficulties with a noisy, aggressive little white dog, which was guarding a jacket. Mr Polly charged him noth-ing – he never thought of it.

A large cloud collected over the inn behind us, and there was a coppery light below the cloud and a cool wind blew, and I talked to the ferryman about the deterioration of our summers. He set me down at the causeway on the rather drea-ry-looking shore of the Swale by the side of Faversham creek.

Arthur D. Lewis

ORDNANCE MAPS AND OTHER THINGS

At Debtling, 'a barren place of chalky, stony soil,' Higgins led the expedition several miles out of the way in quest of the mansion of a friend of his. He assured us that we were certain of an invitation to dinner. We reached the house only to dis-cover that the proprietor had given orders, if any pilgrims called, to say that he had gone away for several weeks.

I remonstrated with Higgins, not merely for wasting our time on specious objects, but for giving rein to his appetite at this early stage. It seemed ridiculous to me that we should talk about dining when we had only yet accomplished about four miles towards the day's quota. I reminded him that we were due at Wye that evening, and that dinner ought not to be even thought of till we reached Lenham.

Higgins said it was absurd to say that we had only done four miles. He appealed to the Ordnance map. By its measurements

102

MITCHELL FARM, SPELDHURST

the distance completed appeared to be less than three and a half miles. Then he remembered his vow of the previous night, and, striking a match, he ignited the remains of the fatal chart and twisted it into pipe-lights.

Higgins' condemnation of the Ordnance map arose from his taking an unnecessarily extreme view of the situation. I once thought myself that these productions were intended as a guide to tourists, and to be regarded as accurate surveys of the country, and to settle disputes as to boundaries, and so on. Now I know that this is a delusion. I never met anybody who ever found his way to anywhere with the assistance of an Ordnance map. The task would be quite impossible even to one initiated into the cabalistic signs and figures which adorn it. You can easily prove this by examining the section supposed to represent a district with which you are perfectly acquainted. Try and find out some favourite route; you will soon be utterly bewildered as to whether some particular line is a footpath which you take for a short cut, or whether it is the high road, or merely a hedge or ditch, or the line of some extinct underground passage. No sanely constituted court of justice would accept such evidence.

But before your mind becomes unhinged and you resort to extreme measures, after the example of Higgins, I will explain to you the laudable principle which governs the action of the Ordnance department. It is a great and glorious device of our military authorities, worthy of being classed with the grand military stratagems of Caesar, Scipio, or King Alfred. Our War Office have an infallible provision secured against the time when a hostile army lands on the coast of Kent and commences the march upon London. They will never get there,

SANDWICH

103

KINGSDOWN

because their route will be dictated by the Ordnance map. Lost in inextricable mazes, they will wander aimlessly hither and thither, their artillery sunk into some unmarked swamp, their men disorganized and half-starved in the search after inns which are not where they seem to be, the leaders demoralized and bewildered by the surprising alterations in the aspect of the country. Eventually they are sure to fall into ambush and be ignominiously captured or cut to pieces. No true Englishman ought to disparage or abuse the Ordnance map. Rather let him subscribe a fund for the distribution of specially bound and beautifully printed copies among all the nations of the world. The Ordnance map is a splendid institution – but not to guide your footsteps when engaged on a walking tour.

Higgins was in no way comforted by my explanations, and fell back on the plea that he was hungry. I might have ignored his proposal, but alas! he had appealed to the lower passions of the Photographer and the Boy, and I was outvoted. All I could

do was protest against the encouragement of gourmandising, especially on walking tours. Light refreshment is sufficient during the walking hours of the day, with a good square meal at the last stopping place before the journey is over. But Higgins thought differently. Then I resorted to stratagem, and with apparent reluctance moved a resolution that we should dine at the next inn. This was carried with acclamation, my opponents falling readily into the trap. We ordered dinner at the next inn; to the horror of Higgins bread and cheese were the only eatables obtainable! I had stooped to conquer. An enormous cheese was placed before us, a very diminutive one left the table; Higgins consoling himself in quantity for what the repast lacked in quality. A new beer cask was also needed before we departed, in spite of my admonitions in praise of moderation.

H. Parr

ST MICHAEL'S, TENTERDEN

THE WAYS OF THE WEALD

The Weald of Kent is the region, once thickly wooded and an almost impenetrable wild, lying between the ragstone ridge south of Maidstone and a line drawn from Ashurst to Dungeness, excluding the marshes within six or eight miles of the sea. This is only approximate, the exact limits of the Weald having been the subject of numerous lawsuits on the subject of tithe and the felling of timber. It has been contended that the Pilgrims' Way on the chalk hills of the North Downs is the northern limit. These are known as the White Hills, whereas the ragstone ridge are called the Red Hills. A celebrated case was fought out, dragging on for a period of ten years, on the question of wood tithe. The Weald of Kent was exempt from a tithe on wood, and the crux of the whole case was whether a certain wood near Aylesford was within the boundaries of the Weald of Kent or not. If the Red Hills formed the boundary this wood did not come within the exempted area, and the Vicar of Aylesford was right in claiming tithe. The Vicar's counsel, addressing the jury, said –

> The Chalk Hills will enclose within the Weald the towns of Maidstone and Malling. Lord Stanhope, who professes great knowledge on the subject, says that the Weald means a Wild, and my learned friend, the Solicitor-General, who has been studying the Saxon language for the purpose of this cause, tells you that a Weald is nothing more or less than an immense wilderness, impervious

to man or beast. If that is so, it is a very odd and extra-ordinary thing that Maidstone, which is the capital of Kent, should have been situate in a place impervious to the approach of man or beast!

Since this famous case the Red Hills have been regarded as the northernmost limit of the Weald.

The fact that nearly all buildings in this forest region must have been of wood accounts for the scarcity of architectural traces of great age except in the churches. The nature of the country, too, has been changed since the land has been cleared and brought into cultivation. We must remember that this was the iron country of the Elizabethan age.

It is probable that one day, if we are to trust the analogies of history, artists and poets will be rambling among the slag heaps of Sheffield or the waste places of Nuneaton, seeking inspiration. They will delight in the rich verdure of steep declivities. They will select picturesque 'bits' suitable for the landscape of the Royal Academy of 3021 among the well-wooded vales, or write odes to nightingales in the solemn stillness of the forest glades. Perhaps some archaeologist will remind them that these rural haunts were not designed to be holiday haunts, and the tumbled appearance of the primrose-covered banks was the result of man's work and not Nature's; that these woodlands were once regions of roaring industry, of furnace glare and belching smoke of fierce labour disputes, of strikes, and the unceasing struggle between capital and labour.

KNOCKWOOD, TENTERDEN

Time was when the very heart of the Garden of England, the Weald of Kent, was (together with the adjacent Weald of Sussex) the black country of our land. The dense forests of this district yielded fuel for the furnaces. The iron-stone could be had for the asking on the surface (the numerous pits, now generally ponds, abound in a hundred unexpected places still), and charcoal was easily made. Thus the ironmasters flourished. It was coal, elsewhere, that was the death of the charcoal process.

D. Maxwell

THE PASSING HOURS

Villagers are very skilful in knowing the time without referring either to clock or watch, and their wits are especially keen when the dinner-hour is approaching.

They are always remarkable prophets concerning the weather and the changes in the direction of the wind. They watch the vane on the church spire, and homely rhymes enable them to prophesy what the weather will be. Thus the peasant tells:

> When the wind is north-west
> The weather is at the best;
> If the rain comes out of the east,
> 'Twill rain twice twenty-four hours at the least.

Another rhyme assures us:

> A southerly wind with showers of rain,
> Will bring the wind from west again.

The north wind brings snow, wet, and cold. A north-east wind is neither good for man nor beast. But

> The wind in the west
> Suits every one best.

The villagers can tell the kind of weather to be expected from watching the animals, who are famous prophets. Thus an ass's bray foretells rain. The bees stay at home when it is likely to be wet. A crowing cock at even, or a bawling peacock, prognosticates rain. High-flying rooks or low-flying swallows predict bad weather; and

> When black snails cross your path
> Black clouds much moisture hath.

Whatever may be the value of this weather-wisdom, the vane on the church spire never lies. It is a beautiful and graceful object, which again bears witness to the skill of the village blacksmith. Its form is traditional, and has been handed down to our own day from the time of St Dunstan. Its popular name weather-cock suggests its shape. Why was this bird selected to preside over our spires and turrets? It is the emblem of vigilance.

P.H. Ditchfield

THE STORYTELLER

THE MEN OF KENT v. THE KENTISH MEN

Canterbury, too, claims to be in a special sense, the city of the men of Kent. There has been so much discussion as to who are men of Kent and who are Kentish men that it seems appropriate here to give the best opinion obtainable on that subject. Some say that those west of the Medway are the true men of Kent, and they found their assertion on a tradition that William the Conqueror on marching from Dover, was withstood by the west Kent men at Swanscombe, where, in return for their submission, the new monarch granted them a continuance of their ancient privileges in memory of which the west Kent men were styled the 'men of Kent'. History, however, affords no confirmation of this tradition, but, on the contrary, is distinctly opposed to it. Mr Charles Sandys, FSA, more than half a century ago, dealt with this matter exhaustively in *Notes and Queries*. He says:

That the east Kent people were denominated from ancient time 'men of Kent', may, I think, be inferred from the ancient name of its metropolis, Cantwarabyrig, literally, 'The City of the men of Kent'. The conversion of the Pagan inhabitants of Kent proceeded so rapidly that St Augustine with the assistance of King Ethelbert,

SHELDWICH FORGE

NORTH LANE, CANTERBURY

soon founded another episcopal see at Rochester, and thus divided the Kentish kingdom into two dioceses: the eastern, or diocese of Canterbury, the western or diocese of Rochester, and this, I conceive, originated the divisions of east and west Kent, the men of the former retaining their ancient name of 'men of Kent', while those of the latter adopted that of 'Kentish men'.

In proof that the divisions of east and west Kent are of very ancient date there is a deed in the archives of Canterbury Cathedral referring to certain property as having been that of 'Oswulf, Duke and Prince of the province of East Kent', about the year 844. The Anglo-Saxon Chronicle, under date A.D. 852, mentions that the 'men of Kent' fought in Thanet against the Danes. In the same record, under date A.D. 865 it is written 'This year the heathen army sat down in Thanet and made peace with the men of Kent.' Further, under date A.D. 999, when there was fighting between the Danes and the Kentish forces at Rochester, it is written, 'full nigh all the west Kentishmen were ruined.' This seems good evidence that long before the Conquest the inhabitants of East Kent were called 'men of Kent', and that at the same period those who dwelt by the Medway were referred to as 'Kentish men', and as there is nothing opposed to this except a later tradition which has no historic confirmation, it may be accepted that Canterbury is truly the City of the 'men of Kent'.

T. Bavington Jones

BRENZETT CHURCH

RAMSGATE

SNIPPETS

The air of this district (Tenham) has long been regarded as unhealthy, from the marshy land which lies to the north. Three parishes are specially condemned in an old local rhyme:

He that will not live long,
Let him dwell at Murston, Tenham, or Tong.

From an old local rhyme it would seem that Dartford formerly bore no enviable character.

Sutton for mutton, Kirby for beef,
South Darent for gingerbread, and Dartford for a thief.

Ramsgate capons, Peter's lings,
Broadstear scrubs, and Meregate kings.

Black's Guide to Kent

Rye, Romney and Hythe, for wealth without health,
The Downs for health with poverty;
But you shall find both health and wealth
From Foreland Head to Knole and Lee.

Anon.

CORONATION DECORATIONS, DARTFORD

THE KILL

WILD LIFE

These badgers must indeed have possessed an amazing strength to make their earth in such a place. The trunks and low horizontal branches of the elder bushes had been used, some to rub their hide on and some to clean their clay-covered feet, so that some were rubbed smooth and others plastered with clay. The floors of the burrows as far down as one could see and feel were thickly carpeted with freshly gathered moss, carried down to form the nest.

It struck me very forcibly when viewing this earth, and thinking of its occupant's tremendous power, tenacity, and hardiness, and of his excessive shyness and strictly nocturnal habits, that, in spite of his rarity, he may yet win in the race of life with his more numerous and protected neighbour, the fox. That fox-hunting will eventually die out as a national sport in this country is now a common belief even among those who pursue it with the greatest enthusiasm; and when that time arrives there will be nothing to save the fox from the fate of the wolf, the marten, and the wild cat; unless indeed a new sentiment should spring up in the place of the existing one to preserve him as a member of the British fauna – a sentiment similar to that which has preserved the useless heron in this country, and is now saving the golden eagle from extermination in the north of Scotland. It is so easy to kill the fox, and he is such a destructive beast, that half a century hence we can imagine the farmer and henwife saying, 'If the fox is wanted alive for the sake of his beauty, or for some such reason, the good people who want him must pay for his keep, otherwise it must be a life for a life.'

But the badger is not destructive; or at all events the damage he inflicts on the farmer is comparatively insignificant, and he is very very hard to kill. Though our largest savage beast he has, up till now, maintained his existence throughout the length and breadth of the land, in spite of much persecution; and we now see that there is growing up a feeling in favour of his preservation, which will make his position safer.

I learned on inquiry that the badgers whose earth I had found were not in any danger of being disturbed, and I was told of a second earth a few miles from the first where the animals were also allowed to be at peace.

W.H. Hudson

CONNAUGHT PARK, DOVER

THE CINQUE PORT

Below the down the stranded town
What may betide forlornly waits,
With memories of smoky skies,
When Gallic navies crossed the straits:
When waves with fire and blood grew bright,
And cannon thundered through the night.

With swinging stride the rhythmic tide
Bore to the harbour barque and sloop;
Across the bar the ship of war,
In castled stern and lanterned poop,
Came up with conquests on her lee,
The stately mistress of the sea.

Where argosies have wooed the breeze,
The simple sheep are feeding now;
And near and far across the bar
The ploughman whistles at the plough;
Where once the long waves washed the shore,
Larks from their lowly lodgings soar.

Below the down the stranded town
Hears far away the rollers beat;
About the wall the seabirds call;
The salt wind murmurs through the street;
Forlorn the sea's forsaken bride
Awaits the end that shall betide.

John Davidson (1857–1909)

MRS BETTS' ILLNESS

During the autumn of 1892, Mrs Betts suffered from an attack of inflammation of the lungs, and when somewhat recovered was advised to seek change in a milder climate. The closing days of that year and the spring of 1893 were passed at St Leonards-on-Sea; and towards summer it was a simple natural transition to move to the more bracing air of Tunbridge Wells. The next step was to the neighbouring village of Pembury, where respectable lodgings were found – recommended by the landlady of the Camden who was not able to receive Mr and Mrs Betts at the hotel as they had hoped – and where there

113

TUNBRIDGE WELLS

was suitable accommodation for the servants and horses in the event of their going abroad. The rooms at Harcourt House were small and low, so that at first they were reluctant to remain more than one night; but, though perfectly unconscious of the fact, they were led to the very spot which was to be the sphere of their future life and labours, and they were constrained to stay there.

On their return from abroad, Mr and Mrs Betts engaged two extra rooms, and invited their beloved Quaker friend, Benjamin B. Wiffen, to visit them. This he did on two occasions; and during these lengthy sojourns at Pembury, by the joint assistance of Mr and Mrs Betts – the former translating his quotations, and the latter acting as his amanuensis – he was enabled to accomplish the desire of his heart in helping to bring out the modern translation of the 'CX. Considerations' appending thereto his life of the author.

Thus from Pembury went forth the English version of the writings of God's faithful servant, so aptly described by Charles H. Spurgeon as 'a resurrection after a burial of three hundred years'. At the back of Pembury new church runs the private Camden road to Bayham Abbey, a charmingly secluded spot, and called by the three friends the 'Alameda' (the Spanish name for a promenade); to this did they daily resort for rest and exercise after work, and referring to this happy time Benjamin B. Wiffen writes as follows:

'Aided by my excellent amanuensis, I sketched out my plan, nor had I occasion once to vary it. Every day witnessed our pleasant progress. The hours of composition, of study, or of writing, were only interrupted by charming drives in the romantic neighbourhood of Tunbridge Wells; for we were set-

tled for the summer months at a cottage in a primitive village almost within sight of that fashionable town.'

Mr and Mrs Betts, having found the ignorance existing in the village to be very great, were stirred up to do something to remedy it. By the help of friends, amongst whom were Mr Joshua Wilson, Mr John Morley, Mr Samuel Morley, Mr John Crisp (whose mother was a Dickenson), and Mr Benjamin Veness, who offered a piece of ground for the purpose, they built the British School.

So much was this appreciated, especially by Non-Conformists, who objected to having their children taught the Church of England catechism, that the first donation of £1 was offered by a working man, a Wesleyan.

The school was built under the superintendance of the late Mr John Finch of Tunbridge Wells, whilst Mr and Mrs Betts were in Spain. On their return, they found the school opened and in working order, under the charge of a certificated governess (selected by Mr Finch) from the British and Foreign Trading School.

At this juncture a little freehold property was offered for sale on Pembury Upper Green; this they purchased and enlarged, removing their furniture from the Pantechnicon just before the fatal fire, which proved so disastrous to many. Thus commenced a residence destined to be a channel of blessing to those around, and becoming ever richer by. Many earnest workers, both in the world of letters and in fields of Christian labour, found their way to the quiet village, and the bright home – well called 'Sunnyside' – where loving welcome and hospitality ever awaited them.

M. Betts

114

CHIDDINGSTONE

'RESTORATION'

This part of Kent has, perhaps, undergone less change than any other district within the same distance of the metropolis. The villages here have still their modest wayside inns and rose embowered cottages. The dells are so calm and lovely, that the nymphs of the antique world might make them their haunt –

> Jam Cytherea choros ducit Venue imminente Luna;
> Junctaeque Nymphis Gratiae decentes
> Alterno terram quatiunt pede –

without any fear of being disturbed by the intrusion of profane mortals. No glaring erections of laths and stucco disfigure the fairest nooks, and raise their gaunt and hideous turrets amid 'the low and bloomed foliage'. The gray weatherbeaten churches have escaped indecent 'restoration'; 'the forefathers of the hamlet' lie in daisied graveyards, not in joint-stock-company cemeteries. The leviathan of steam has not yet crushed out the poetry and romance of this sweet countryside. Not that we are insensible of the great advantages which increased facilities of communication necessarily induce; but we know that in the neighbourhood of a railway station the village soon swells into a town, the wayside inn grows into a

CROCKHURST

115

THRESHING

railway hotel, the leafy lanes are metamorphosed into the hardest of macadamized roads, and all that makes the life, and magic, and beauty of an English landscape, gradually but surely passes away for ever.

So to these quiet hamlets on this goodly Kentish ridge, retaining in their names such distinct memories of Old England's past – of the Saxon thegn and the Norman baron – to these breezy uplands and leafy coppices, as yet unchanged and unpolluted, we bid the tourist – Welcome! Let us, therefore, continue the diversion we have commenced from our main route, and keep across the hills to Charing.

Black's Guide to Kent

AN OLD KENT PROVERB

> Health without wealth:
> Wealth without health:
> Wealth with health.

According to an old proverb, Kent has been divided into three parts as above.

The cold and dreary marshes of the Thames and Medway, producing excellent pasture, but in former days being very bad for the ague, were designated 'Wealth and no health.'

The high chalk hills, with their barren soil but bracing air, were renowned for 'Health and no wealth.'

116

HIGH STREET, BROMLEY

The sandstone ranges of the Weald, with their smiling valleys, fertile fields and pine and oak-clad hills, still offer both 'Health and Wealth.'

According to another authority, however, 'Health without wealth' refers to East Kent, which is 'pleasant and healthy but with much poor land': 'Wealth without health' is the characteristic of the Weald and Romney Marsh 'famous for its fine pastures and its rich farmers, but extremely liable to ague': while the portion blessed with 'Health and Wealth' is 'that part of Kent nearest London, where the situation is healthy, the soil good, and the inhabitants rich.'

Anonymous

WHEN I WAS YOUNG

I was very young in those days, yet one event is marked in my memory. Being the eldest child, it amused my father and mother to teach me all sorts of things, including games. Backgammon I knew well, and one day Sir Gordon, who was fond of the game, said he would play with me. To be the right height I sat on the round bolster of a sofa – on the sofa. The game was played with much spirit, and I won. Sir Gordon stood up and said:

'Dammy! The child's won the game.'

'Dammy! I have,' I said, delighted, standing up on the sofa, waving the dice-box. If a shell had exploded in the drawing-

117

CHARING

room, a greater shock could not have occurred. I was hustled off the sofa. It was such a delicate point – the language a commodore might use, and a little girl might not. Emily and I were told it was bed-time, and I was taken home by the boatswain. But though Emily and I discussed the matter, we came to no conclusion why we were sent off so quickly. It was only years afterwards, when Lady Bremer herself told me the story, that I understood my breach of manners. She was not then Lady Bremer. Sir Gordon was dead, and she had married an Italian gentleman, and was called Donna Jemima Angiolini Clericetti, a name that I found very difficult to master, and which she allowed me to shorten to Donna Jemima.

'Such language from little lips,' she said, 'quite took one's breath away. What could any one say when dear Sir Gordon had just used the word? My dear! I shall never forget that evening!' and then she laughed. At the time it was no laughing matter.

Jane Connolly

POTIONS

Somewhere about the middle fifties of last century Dr Gorham had a patient at Hadlow or East Peckham (I forget which), who one day ran short of medicine and wished to have his stock replenished. He directed one of his farm hands, a simple, slow-minded creature, to knock off work early and take a horse and ride into Tonbridge to get another bottle. On his arrival the genial doctor was temporarily absent and the surgery was in charge of a young assistant or dispenser who was a cheerful soul and loved a mild practical joke. Telling Hodge to take a seat while 'the mixture as before' was being put up, he presently suggested that he should fetch his visitor a tankard of bitter to beguile the waiting time. Needless to say, the offer met with Hodge's cordial approval, and Mr de Spencer went to the kitchen, taking with him, unobserved, a pinch of powdered jalap to flavour the drink. The medicine was slowly concocted and the beer was gradually consumed, both operations being finished at the same time. The bottle

118

ROSE'S TEA WAREHOUSE, SANDWICH

THE HARBOUR, DOVER

was wrapped in nice white paper and Hodge got ready to go. As he was leaving, Mr de Spencer gave him a word of friendly caution: 'Look here, John, you'll have to be careful with that physic, it's rather strong.'

Hodge was duly grateful: 'All right, sir; thank 'ee, sir.'

'If I were you I wouldn't put the bottle in my pocket. Hold it out at arm's length, as far away from you as you can.'

Hodge mounted his nag and rode under the archway into the High Street, and turned down Swan Lane gingerly grasping the potent mixture with his right arm extended horizontally to its utmost stretch. Before he reached Tile-Barn corner his limb became still and he rested the bottle momentarily on the saddle before him. As he did so, his belief in the young doctor's prescience grew definitely stronger and the arm speedily resumed its previous attitude. Hodge trotted steadily homeward, but before he got to Three Elm Lane he was thoroughly convinced that Mr de Spencer's remarks had been an understatement of the case. He reached a timely hop-garden, descended carefully from his mount, and deposited his uncanny burden gently on the green-sward. Then he climbed over the hedge and disappeared from view. . . . When he emerged, he was carrying a fourteen-foot chestnut pole, of which he had taken larcenous possession and to the extreme end of which he cautiously tied the bottle with his red kerchief. Hodge finished his journey like a mediaeval knight, with his lance sloped gracefully outward and with a scarlet pennon fluttering gaily in the evening breeze.

A.H. Neve

DOVER BEACH

The sea is calm to-night.
The tide is full, the moon lies fair
Upon the straits — on the French coast the light
Gleams and is gone; the cliffs of England stand,
Glimmering and vast, out in the tranquil bay.
Come to the window, sweet is the night-air!
Only, from the long line of spray
Where the sea meets the moon-blanch'd land,
Listen! you hear the grating roar
Of pebbles which the waves draw back, and fling,
At their return, up the high strand,
Begin, and cease, and then again begin,
With tremulous cadence slow, and bring
The eternal note of sadness in.

Sophocles long ago
Heard it on the Aegean, and it brought
Into his mind the turbid ebb and flow
Of human misery; we
Find also in the sound a thought,
Hearing it by this distant northern sea.

The Sea of Faith
Was once, too, at the full, around earth's shore
Lay like the folds of a bright girdle furl'd.
But now I only hear
Its melancholy, long, withdrawing roar,

MATES SCHOOL

Retreating, to the breath
Of the night-wind, down the vast edges drear
And naked shingles of the world.

Ah, love, let us be true
To one another! for the world, which seems
To lie before us like a land of dreams,
So various, so beautiful, so new,
Hath really neither joy, nor love, nor light,
Nor certitude, nor peace, nor help for pain;
And we are here as on a darkling plain
Swept with confused alarms of struggle and flight,
Where ignorant armies clash by night.

Matthew Arnold

THE LITTLE SISTER

In a couple of years Ansdore's credit once more stood high at
Lewes Old Bank, and Ellen could be sent to a select school at
Folkestone – so select indeed that there had been some difficulty about getting her father's daughter into it. Joanna was
surprised as well as disgusted that the schoolmistress should
give herself such airs, for she was very plainly dressed, whereas
Joanna had put on all her most gorgeous apparel for the inter-
view; but she had been very glad when her sister was finally
accepted as a pupil at Rose Hill House, for now she would
have as companions the daughters of clergymen and squires,
and learn no doubt to model herself on their refinement. She
might even be asked to their homes for her holidays, and,
making friends in their circle, take a short cut to silken immo-
bility on the drawing-room sofa by way of marriage . . .
Joanna congratulated herself on having done very well for
Ellen, though during the first weeks she missed Ellen's dainti-
ness at meals, though she had often smacked it – she missed
her strutting at her side to church on Sunday – she missed her
noisy, remonstrant setting out to school every morning and
her noisy affectionate return – her heart ached when she
looked at the little empty bed in her room, and being senti-
mental she often dropped a tear where she used to drop a kiss
on Ellen's pillow.

Sheila Kaye-Smith

121

GOUDHURST

CRANBROOK

Sources & Photographic Details

ACKNOWLEDGEMENTS

I wish to acknowledge the help, advice and support I have received from the following in the compilation of this book. Without their encouragement and knowledge, so willingly given on every occasion, this publication would not have been possible.

Kent County Council Arts Libraries and the Directory of Arts and Libraries, Mr Yinnon Ezra, together with staff of the many libraries contacted and visited in connection with this book; the County Record Office, County Hall, Maidstone; the County Reference Library, and the manager and staff of the Local Studies Centre, County Hall, Maidstone; Ashford Central Library; Folkestone Central Library; Gillingham Library; Gravesend Library; Lydd Library; Sevenoaks Central Library; Sittingbourne Central Library; Sheerness Library; Tenterden Library; Tunbridge Wells Central Library; Bexhill Library; Bromley Central Library (Leisure Services); Hastings Library; Dartford Borough Council (Dartford Museum); Dover District Council (Dover Museum); Miss B. Mason, Curator Bexhill Museum, for the use of their library; Ms Victoria Williams, curator of Hastings Museum for the use of the George Woods collection of photographs; Dr Burgess, Curator of Tenterden Museum and Tenterden Historical Society; Brenchley and Matfield Local History Society, for the use of their photographs; University of Reading (Photographic Department); Mr Martin Hawkins (Sheerness Dockyard); Leeds Castle Foundation; Hever Castle Ltd; The Historic Dockyard, Chatham; Whitbread Hop Farm, Paddock Wood; Sussex Archaeological Society; *Kent* (Magazine) by kind permission of the editor and Men of Kent and Kentish Men; Courier Group Newspapers; Kent Messenger Group Newspapers; Mrs Margot Bennett; Mr and Mrs Denys Blackburn for the loan of his great-grandfather's *Memoirs* (The Hon. Revd Edward Vesey Bligh), for a more detailed account of these, please see *This Was a Man* by Esmé Cecil Wingfield-Stratford; Mrs R. Wingfield-Stratford-Johnstone for permission to quote from her father's book, *Before the Lamps Went Out*; Mrs David Rogers, for permission to use photographs from the Gertrude Rogers Collection; Mr Edward Carpenter, for the loan of photographs; K. Chalmers-Dixon; Mr E.J. Sidery, for permission to use pictures from Boyer's photographic collection; Dr John Whyman, University of Kent, for recommending many of the books perused in compiling the text; George Sassoon, for permission to use text from *Memoirs of a Fox-Hunting Man*, by Siegfried Sassoon; A.P. Watt Ltd, for permission to use text from *Kipps* by H.G. Wells; Random Century Group, for permission to use text from *Unknown Kent* by Donald Maxwell. While every effort has been made to contact all copyright holders, both authors and publishers, in some instances this has proved impossible and to them I apologize. I hope that they will accept this book as a tribute to all those Kent authors of the past, without whom none of this would have been possible.

KENT 100 YEARS AGO

All the page numbers given below relate to pages in this book, and not the page numbers of the source books.

T. Bavington Jones *Pikes New Century Series* pp. 11, 101, 107; The *Invicta Magazine* vols I, II, III: Hal O'Thanet p. 13, F.C. Elliston-Erwood p. 25, Geo. Smith p. 31, Sidney Bredgar p. 35, Anon p. 45, Will Syms p. 55, Philo Cantii p. 62; H.G. Wells *Kipps* pp. 15, 50; The *Kentish Notebook* vols I, II: 'Interested' p. 16, D. Lee p. 100; *Black's Guide to Kent* pp. 16, 110, 115; Rudyard Kipling *Puck of Pook's Hill* p. 18; Lady Hope *English Homes and Villages* p. 20; John Coker Egerton *Sussex Folk and Sussex Ways* pp. 22, 37, 94; A.G. Bradley *England's Outpost* pp. 22, 28, 36, 48, 52, *An Old Gate of England* p. 90; Jane Connolly *Old Days and Old Ways* pp. 24, 54, 117; Arthur D. Lewis *The Kent Coast* pp. 26, 30, 86, 102; P.H. Ditchfield *The Cottage and the Village* p. 27; Louis J. Jennings *Field Paths and Green Lanes* pp. 32, 82; Charles Igglesden *A Saunter through Kent with Pen and Pencil* (various volumes) pp. 33, 40, 70; The *Maidstone and Kent County Standard* 15 October 1881 pp. 34, 38, 57; *The Kentish Note Book*: Mc.B. p. 38, 'Rambler' p. 70; Frederick G. Kitton *Life of Dickens* p. 42; E.V. Lucas *Highways and Byways of Sussex* p. 43; Sheila Kaye-Smith *Joanna Godden* pp. 43, 121; J. Shaw *Travels in England* pp. 45, 92; Richard Jefferies *The Open Air* p. 48; E. Harvey Darton *A Parcel of Kent* p. 57; E.C. Wingfield-Stratford *When the Lamps Went Out* p. 58; Siegfried Sassoon *Memoirs of a Foxhunting Man* p. 60; The Hon. Revd Edward Vesey Bligh *Memoir* pp. 63, 64; Charles Dickens *Great Expectations* p. 69; Walter Jerrold *Highways and Byways in Kent* p. 71; Richard Stead *Bygone Kent* p. 71; Frank Watts *Sussex County Magazine* p. 76; J.Y. Stratton *Hops and Hop Pickers* p. 76; Charles G. Harper and J.C. Earnshaw *The Downs and the Sea* pp. 78, 89; Edwin Harris *Kentish Customs* p. 83; H, Parr *New Wheels in Old Ruts* pp. 83, 102; Walter Dexter *The Kent of Dickens* (story told by George Dolby of Reading Tours) p. 84; P.H. Ditchfield *The Charm of the English Garden* pp. 88, 106, *The Cottage and Life of Rural England* p. 90; A.F. Abell *History of Kent* p. 89; D. Maxwell *Unknown Kent* pp. 92, 97, 105; A.H. Neve *The Tonbridge of Yesterday* pp. 95, 118; R. Thurston Hopkins *Sheila Kaye-Smith and the Weald Country* p. 95; W.H. Hudson *Nature in Downland* p. 112; J. Davidson *The Cinque Port* p. 113; M. Betts *The Dickensons* p. 113; Anon *Kent* (Magazine) p. 116; Matthew Arnold *Dover Beach* p. 120.

ILLUSTRATIONS

The credits and information on all the illustrations used in this book are given in page ascending sequence. Where a source is referred to frequently only initials are used, and the key to these is at the end of this section. Where dates are known, or reasonably easily deduced by the owners of the pictures, they have been given. Many of the photographs reproduced here that are held by Hastings Museum are from the George Woods collection; he was an outstanding Victorian photographer born in 1852. In the late 1880s George moved to Hastings, spending much of his time taking pictures of the Sussex and Kent countryside. He died in 1934 and his second wife, Ethel, gave his collection of photographs to Hastings Museum. I am extremely grateful to the museum for the use of their property. Also I am deeply grateful to Mr E.J. Sidery for the use of the Sidery Collection, consisting of the photographs of William Henry Boyer (1827–97) Master Photographer of Sandwich from 1868 to 1897. A man of considerable talent, Boyer operated in Sandwich and the surrounding district at a time when photography was in its infancy, requiring the photographer to have the specialist knowledge and skill to prepare his own glass plates from the raw chemicals. The collection consists of some three thousand plates, numbered and indexed, which lay undisturbed in the attic of Boyer's studio until the premises were sold in 1971, when Mr E.A. Sidery, who had bought the business from one of Boyer's successors in 1914, retired at the age of ninety-one. The plates passed in due course to Mr Sidery's son, Mr E.J. Sidery, who is the present owner. Another valuable collection of photographs is that held by the Local Studies Centre, County Hall, Maidstone and to them I am duly grateful.

Front cover, The bridge, Eynsford; *AG.* Front endpaper, Shop of F. Durrant, Grocer of Sandwich, *c.* 1880; *EJS.* Back endpaper, High Street, Rochester, *c.* 1905; *AG.* Page (i), Fishmarket, Folkestone, *c.* 1900; *AG.* Page (ii), Groombridge, 1890; *HM.* Woman carrying water, *c.* 1890; *HM.* Page (iii), Buckland Brewery, London Road *c.* 1880; *Dover District Council (Dover Museum).* In the foreground is the Buckland brick-field; at rear is Kingsfords Buckland Brewery, closed 1890, which incorporated the Buckland windmill, built 1795. All demolished in the 1960s. Page (iv), Lifeboat Saturday, Sittingbourne, 1904; *Sittingbourne Library.* Page 1, Smallthythe (yeoman's house), *c.* 1880; *HM.* Page 2, Honor's Forage Works, Maidstone, *c.* 1890. LSC. Page 3, Cottage near Horsmonden, *AG.* Page 4, Leeds Castle, *c.* 1908; *Leeds Castle Foundation & University of Reading.* Page 5, A 17 lb cabbage. E.J. Mercer, Greengrocer & Fruiterer, High Street, Tenterden, *c.* 1914; *Tenterden and Ashford Libraries.* On the left is John Mercer and on the right Charles Mercer. Page 6, Cutting Wood, *c.* 1890; *H.M.* Wagoner & team, *c.* 1880; *EJS.* Page 7, Church Hill, Beckenham *c.* 1904; *AG.* Asleep in the hop garden, *c.* 1880; *EJS.* Page 8, Margate, *c.* 1900; *LSC (KCC).* Page 9, Girl at the well, Cobham farmyard 1861; *Mrs David Rogers and the KCC Arts and Libraries Department.* Page 10, Advertisement from *Thomson's Local Directory and Almanac, 1890* for Tenterden Brewery. Page 11, Milsted; *AG.* Page 12, King's Head Inn, Sissinghurst, *c.* 1910; *AG.* Page 13, Marden, *c.* 1905; *AG.* Page 14, Ramsgate Harbour, 1900; *LSC (KCC).* Page 15, Fishermen at Deal, *c.* 1905; *LSC (KCC).* Page 16, Hythe Canal, *c.* 1920; *AG.* Page 17, Rochester Cathedral and Castle, *c.* 1905; *LSC (KCC).* Rochester Castle; *AG.* Page 18, A dyke on Romney Marsh, *c.* 1890; *HM.* Wittersham, *c.* 1890; *HM.* Page 19, Brookland church, *c.* 1890; *HM.* Page 20, Old Priory & church, New Romney, *c.* 1905; *AG.* Page 21, The Pantiles, Tunbridge Wells; *AG.* Page 22, 'Hoppers', *c.* 1925; *AG.* Page 23, The Street, Wingham, *c.* 1905; *AG.* East Kent Colliery, Eythorne; *AG.* Page 24, May Day celebration, *c.* 1910; *AG.* Page 25, Mrs Caroline Gibbs of Elmstone and customers, *c.* 1880; *EJS.* Page 26, Coopers, *c.* 1880; *EJS.* Page 27, The Tudor Gateway, Rochester, *c.* 1860; *Mrs David Rogers and KCC Arts and Libraries Department.* Page 28, Sheep shearing team, *c.* 1910; *Edward Carpenter.* Page 29, Fairfold church, Romney Marsh, *c.* 1890; *HM.* Page 30, The Lees, Folkestone, *c.* 1903; *Folkestone Library.* Page 31, Folkestone Harbour; *AG.* Page 32, Hever Castle, *c.* 1910; *Hever Castle Ltd.* Page 33, The Town Hall, Fordwich, *c.* 1910; *AG.* Page 34, Master Kelly, fruiterer. *c.* 1885; *EJS.* Page 35, Winter landscape – exact location unknown, *c.* 1890; *HM.* Page 36, Margate, Queens Promenade, *c.* 1905; *AG.* Page 37, Cricket Week, The Pantiles, Tunbridge Wells; *AG.* Page 38, Aveling and Porter 8 h.p. traction engine built around 1888 and owned by William Lambert of Horsmonden, delivering coal from Paddock Wood Station to Brenchley; *Brenchley and Matfield Local History Association.* Page 39, Two children in pram outside St Bart's Almshouses, Sandwich; *EJS.* Page 40, Scything; *Sussex Archaeological Society.* William Sutton, gardener, 1880; *EJS.* Page 41, Reaping; *AG.* Page 42, Sunday morning, Chatham Barracks, *c.* 1905; *AG.* Page 43, Toad Rock at Rusthall, near Tunbridge Wells; *HM.* Page 44, Church interior at Ivychurch, *c.* 1890; *HM.* Page 45, High Street, Tunbridge Wells, *c.* 1905; *AG.* Page 46, The Pantiles, Tunbridge Wells; *AG.* Page 47, The Common, Tunbridge Wells, *c.* 1900; *HM.* Page 48, Cherry pickers; *Ashford Library.* Page 49, Bleak House, Broadstairs; *AG.* Page 50, Oyster fishermen, Whitstable; *AG.* Page 51, Snargate, *c.* 1890;

HM. Tricycle outside Wakefield's shop, Sandwich; *EJS.* Page 52, Canterbury Cathedral in the background, *c.* 1900; *AG.* Page 53, The Market, Canterbury; *AG.* High Street, Canterbury; *AG.* Page 54, Lamberhurst looking north, *c.* 1885; *HM.* Page 55, Servants, *c.* 1880, may have worked for a family named Hooper; *EJS.* Page 56, Railway workers, *c.* 1880; *EJS.* Page 57, Hop pickers at Yalding, *c.* 1905; *AG.* Page 58, Dockyard workers, Chatham, *c.* 1910; *AG.* Page 59, St Mary's church and Gun Wharf, Chatham; *AG.* Page 60, The carrier's van, may be at Eastry; *EJS.* Page 61, Wattle load at corner of Galliard Street and King Street, Sandwich, *c.* 1885; *EJS.* Birling; *Mrs Pamela Blackburn.* Page 62, Aylesford Bridge, Aylesford, near Maidstone; *AG.* Page 63, Lych Gate, Buckland church, Dover, *c.* 1900; *AG.* The Hon. Revd Edward Vesey Bligh and family, 1862; *Mr & Mrs Denys Blackburn.* Page 64, Cobham Hall (built *c.* 1590 and altered eighty years later), *c.* 1890 *KCC LSC.* Page 65, Market Square, Dover, *c.* 1906; *Dover District Council (Dover Museum).* Page 66, Malling Road, Snodland, *c.* 1910; *AG.* Page 67, High Street, Rochester; *AG.* Riverside scene, *c.* 1885; *HM.* Page 68, The boys' playground; *HM.* Page 69, Ruckinge church, Romney Marsh. *c.* 1890; *HM.* Page 70, Hunt at Appledore, *c.* 1912; Ashford Library. Page 71, The Reculver, near Herne Bay; *AG.* Page 72, North Street, Ashford; *AG.* Page 73, The pea pickers, *c.* 1885; *EJS.* Page 74, Harbour and Barracks, Dover; *c.* 1905; *AG.* The old hop picker, *c.* 1880; *EJS.* Page 75, Poultry outside Mr Curling's shop, Fisher Street, Sandwich, *c.* 1885; *EJS.* Page 76, A catch of sprats, Deal; *AG.* Page 77, Hop pickers; *Kent and Sussex Courier and Tunbridge Wells Advertiser, and Whitbread Hop Farm.* Page 78, Burning Off; *HM.* Page 79, Homeward Bound; *HM.* Hedging; *HM.* Smallbrook/Speldhurst crossroads; *AG.* Page 80, Horse-drawn van outside Boyer's Photographic Rooms, Sandwich; *EJS.* Two women outside cottage; the figure on the left thought to be Mrs Caroline Gibbs of Elmstone; *EJS.* Page 81, Workmen at Bilsington, *c.* 1890; *HM.* Servant sweeping with a besom; *Brenchley & Matfield Local History Society.* Gardener cutting wood; *Brenchley & Matfield Local History Society.* Page 82, Penshurst; *AG.* Page 83, Lenham; *AG.* Page 84, Near Biddenham; *HM.* Page 85, Pilgrimage to Canterbury; *EJS.* Page 86, On the hills above Snodland; *AG.* Canterbury; *HM.* Page 87, The wreck of the *Mahratta,* 1909; *AG.* Page 88, Cottage near Benenden; *HM.* Page 89, Hop oasts, Barming, and Hunt; *AG.* Kentish Cricketer; *EJS.* Page 90, Stone, Isle of Oxney; *AG.* Page 91, Washerwoman, *c.* 1885; *EJS.* Page 92, The crossroads, unidentified location believed to be near Tunbridge Wells; *HM.* Page 93, The bargeman on river near Maidstone; *HM.* Maidstone Wharf, *c.* 1900; *Sussex Archaeological Society.* Page 94, Mr Body's barge on the river at Smallthythe, *c.* 1900; *AG.* Page 95, Tonbridge School, Tonbridge; *AG.* Page 96, Pope's Gang digging out a dyke on Romney Marsh; *E. Carpenter.* Page 97, The river near Maidstone; *Sussex Archaeological Society.* Page 98, Riverside scene; *HM.* Page 99, Fishing in the lock; *HM.* Believed to be the River Medway; *HM.* Page 100, Hop pickers; *EJS.* Page 101, Shakespeare Cliff, Dover; *AG.* Page 102, Grove Ferry; *AG.* Page 103, Mitchell Farm, Speldhurst; *AG.* Sandwich; *AG.* Page 104, Kingsdown; *AG.* Page 105, St Michael's, Tenterden; *c.* 1910; *Tenterden Museum.* Page 106, Knockwood, Tenterden; *AG.* Page 107, The story-teller, *c.* 1890; *HM.* Sheldwich Forge, *c.* 1920; *AG.* Page 108, North Lane, Canterbury; *AG.* Page 109, Brenzett church, *c.* 1890; *HM.* Page 110, Ramsgate beach, *c.* 1900; *KCC Local Studies Centre.* Page 111, Coronation decorations in Dartford High Street, 26 June 1902; *Dartford Borough Council (Dartford Museum).* Page 112, 'The Kill'; *HM.* Page 113, Connaught Park, Dover; *AG.* Page 114, The Pantiles, Tunbridge Wells; *AG.* Page 115, Chiddingstone, *c.* 1900; *HM.* Crockhurst, *c.* 1920; *AG.* Page 116, Threshing; *EJS.* Page 117, High Street, Bromley; *Leisure Services, Bromley Central Library.* Page 118, Charing; *AG.* Page 119, Rose's Tea Warehouse, King Street, Sandwich; *EJS.* Page 120, Wellington Dock, *c.* 1895, looking east towards Dover Castle; *Dover District Council (Dover Museum).* On the right are the boat-building yards. Page 121, Young croquet players, Mates School, *c.* 1880; *EJS.* Page 122, Goudhurst, *c.* 1900; *KCC LSC.* Cranbrook, with windmill in background, *c.* 1900; *KCC LSC.*

Key: AG, Aylwin Guilmant, author collection. EJS, E.J. Sidery. HM, Hastings Museum. KCC, Kent County Council. LSC, Local Studies Centre.